WOODROW WILSON
From the portrait by Sir William Orpen R. A.

WOODROW WILSON

The Caricature, the Myth and the Man

by

EDITH GITTINGS REID

WW

1934

OXFORD UNIVERSITY PRESS

London New York Toronto

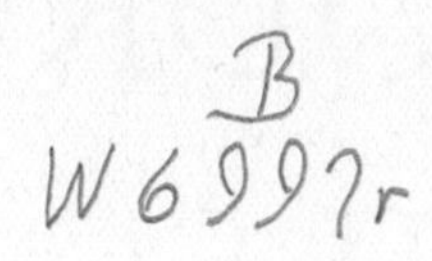

PRINTED IN THE UNITED STATES OF AMERICA

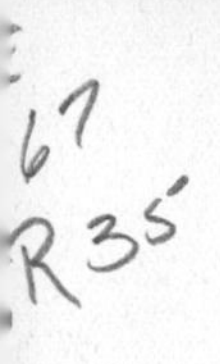

TO

MARGARET WOODROW WILSON

HIS DAUGHTER

AND

HARRY AUGUSTUS GARFIELD

HIS FRIEND

ACKNOWLEDGMENTS

WILSON's early work on government, and his writings and addresses, collected by R. S. Baker and Dodd in the important volumes entitled *The Public Papers of Woodrow Wilson*, give his political creed. The authorized *Life* by Ray Stannard Baker is a rich source of information from all angles. For the interpretation of the official side of Wilson's life I am especially indebted to *Colonel House's Intimate Papers;* and to both Colonel and Professor Charles Seymour for their great kindness and the pains they took to select and send me copies of those letters of Mr. Wilson to Colonel House that seemed to them to touch the high lights of his political life; to Dodd's *Woodrow Wilson and his Work;* to Houston's *Eight Years with the Wilson Cabinet;* to Palmer's *Life of Newton D. Baker;* and to numerous other essays, memoirs, and less comprehensive biographies. Frank Cobb, of the *New York World*, and Walter Lippmann, though they have written little on this subject, have a sure touch when Wilson, the man and politician, is under consideration. I am especially indebted to Mr. Ray Stannard Baker for his courtesy in permitting me to use letters from Mr. Wilson to me which had previously been given to him for his use in his authorized *Life of Woodrow Wilson.* President Harry A. Garfield, of Williams College, gave me every assistance in his power. To Professor William Starr Myers, of Princeton University, my thanks are due for some intimate details. It is impossible to name all who have assisted me, but I must express my thanks to Mr. Bernard M. Baruch for permission to reproduce the unfinished Orpen portrait; and to Miss Harriet W. Frishmuth for the picture of her bust of Woodrow Wilson.

PREFACE

THE Wilson administration occurred during such a period of storm and stress, when all human passions were at the boiling point, that the solitary figure of the advocate of peace became the target both for the mud-slinging and for the eulogies of an abnormal world. He was made either a god upon the mountain to whom all appeals must be made, or else a bloodless pedagogue playing a lone hand in the attic of his own soul, a hindrance and a disturbance rather than a constructive force.

Innumerable articles and reminiscences of Mr. Wilson have been written, and a number of biographies, many of them more autobiographical than biographical; but in the main they have been written by those who knew him only in the latter part of his life, or who knew him personally not at all. Consequently these portrayals depict the president or the statesman rather than the man; and as a rule they are coloured by their authors' political convictions.

This is not an attempt at historical narrative, though it is so intertwined with the political life of the day that one is inevitably drawn with Wilson into big events and made to share his ideas, his politics, his democracy, his personality — he insisted that one should share them. I am not concerned with whether what he did was right or wrong but only with why he did it. Having known him intimately from his youth to his death, my effort is to separate him from the mass of irrelevant matter collected about him, to consider the man alone — his ideas, his purposes, and the motives that controlled him.

It is curious how Abraham Lincoln's simplicity illuminates his character, while Wilson's simplicity bewilders the interpreters of his. The Wilson caricature, made out of hate, without humour, is fast fading away. The myth is growing and obscuring the man. This is ironic, as the object of his life was to make his ideals practicable. My aim is to draw a portrait of the man I knew so well for those who are bewildered by conflicting and untrue accounts of his personality.

The desire of his daughters, Margaret and the late Mrs. Sayre, that I should undertake the characterization of their father was a determining factor. This portraiture gains its authority from our close friendship, long and familiar conversations, and the many letters written to me by Mr. Wilson from his youth to shortly before his death in 1924. Strangely enough there are few great men given to letter-writing whose letters are frankly revealing. Mr. Wilson was among these few. His intimate letters to his friends explain a certain side of his nature and show why his friends cared for him as they did. It is therefore unfortunate that I am not permitted to publish his letters to me or to include in this biography certain of his personal letters to Colonel House, which the latter has so courteously put at my disposal. I have been able to use only a few letters, parts of which have already appeared in Mr. Ray Stannard Baker's biography.

While writing this book I have kept Mr. Wilson's personality ever before me. I may not always remember his exact words but I cannot fail to remember his thought.

> "So word by word, and line by line
> The dead man touched me from the past,
> And all at once it seemed at last
> His living soul was flashed on mine."

EDITH GITTINGS REID

BALTIMORE, NOVEMBER, 1933

CONTENTS

I
BIRTH AND ANTECEDENTS

Out of the blinding swirl of the dust of humanity
emerges an individual

Chapter One

BIRTH AND ANTECEDENTS

THOMAS WOODROW WILSON, who became successively President of Princeton College, Governor of New Jersey, twenty-eighth President of the United States, Founder of the League of Nations, and an inspired voice, persistent and reasoning, pleading, in the midst of turbulence, for peace and fair play, was born on the 12th of December, 1856, at Staunton, Virginia.

His antecedents, on the paternal side, are refreshingly vigorous and effective, but the records only carry us as far back as his grandparents.

In the year 1807 there sailed from Ulster, in a ship bound for the port of Philadelphia in the United States of America, two young emigrants, James Wilson and Anne Adams, both of County Down, Ireland. The boy of twenty was tall, handsome, humorous, enthusiastic, with a genius for life; the girl was sixteen, homely, unhumorous, with an unbreakable will to meet life in an effective practical way. They were the healthiest and least subtle of young animals. Each had an equal zest for achievement; and, though both were grounded and steeped in Presbyterianism, it was neither the missionary spirit nor enthusiasm for a cause that brought them from the old country to the new; it was entirely a determination to get on. Realizing that their goal was the same, namely, to make a substantial living, build a home, have children and establish themselves in a recognized place in the world, they decided that they would work well together and that, just so soon as it was practicable, they would marry. One is glad to be spared the love-making of these two common-sensible young people, though one might not call it romance it was durable emotion and lasted all their lives — and they got on. They stood delightfully assured with their backs to the past, good stuff if a little hard — Scotch-Irish Presbyterians.

As soon as the young emigrants reached Philadelphia, James Wilson obtained work at the office of *The Aurora*, one of the leading newspapers of the city. His energy and common sense, combined with good looks and a genial manner, made a deep impression upon the editor, William Duane, who became his warm friend. Duane preferred him so rapidly that Wilson was soon able to marry; and in five years' time he practically controlled *The Aurora*. Our papers, then as now, gave full vent to political speech and unsuppressed emotions. *The Aurora*, voluble and virulent, did record work in bringing the Democratic Party into power.

Though so prosperous in Philadelphia, James Wilson felt that he could do still better in the West. Accordingly in 1812, with his wife and family he moved to Steubenville, Ohio. The penniless boy of five years ago had now a good bank account and glowing letters of recommendation in his pocket. After settling in Steubenville he became owner of the *Steubenville Gazette* and of the *Pennsylvania Advocate* in Pittsburgh. He threw himself with abandon into the political life of the day, and before his death became a member of the Ohio legislature and an Associate Judge of Common Pleas — a man of substance and a very prominent citizen in a small place. His humour must have been an irresistible force to survive in the atmosphere of that grim dame, his wife, who forged ahead by his side, disciplining their seven sons and three daughters. His famous grandson inherited much of this humour.

The youngest son, Joseph Ruggles, was like his father in temperament; he inherited his vigour and geniality. From his mother came his theological strain without her hardness. Theology with him softened into religion. He learned his father's trade of printer, adding to it a liberal education for that time and place. He took a number of small college honours and he might have become a good journalist or a fluent and successful politician; but theology had taken hold of him and he elected to enter the Presbyterian ministry. Before actually taking a ministerial charge he taught for some years at the Academy in Steubenville; and it was during this time that he met Janet Woodrow, the daughter of a Presbyterian minister. After a more romantic courtship than that of his father and mother, they were married in 1849 at Chillicothe, Ohio, where the Reverend Thomas Woodrow, the bride's father, was pastor of the First Presbyterian Church. Both Thomas Woodrow and his wife were Scotch and had come to settle in America when well advanced in life, and after all their children had been born in Scotland.

Though the paternal grandparents of Woodrow Wilson had practically said, " Go ahead with your hero; he needs no better start than ourselves," the Woodrows, on the other hand, give an alarmingly long pedigree. Its only characteristic of interest to us is the curiously persistent uniformity of the strain: professors, clergymen, gentle gentlemanly men and very feminine women, with strong religious convictions and moral rectitude. There are no bars sinister nor madcap doings in this genealogy; and everywhere, in every direction, you meet the Woodrows in the Presbyterian Church. The tribe might have been more interesting if a few other creeds had been sprinkled in, but there is little doubt that this unmixed strain was responsible for Woodrow Wilson's consistent and permanent convictions.

The humour in the Wilson family came from the paternal grandfather. On the maternal side there was none at all in either male or female line. Janet Woodrow was devoutly religious and a devoted wife and mother, as deeply dyed in Presbyterianism as her mother-in-law. But she was of a gentler nature, firmness taking the place of dominance, controlling her children with persuasion and sympathy, rather than with the rod. She was a cultivated woman who showed traditions of gentle breeding; and though she could not laugh understandingly over the Reverend Joseph's jokes, she could smile when she knew a smile was expected. To her son, Woodrow, who had a good deal of the feminine in him, she was a model of the only type of woman he ever really understood.

In 1855 Joseph Wilson became pastor of the First Presbyterian Church in Staunton, Virginia; and a record tells us that "In the Presbyterian Manse on the 28th day of December, 1856, was born to the Reverend Joseph Ruggles and Janet Woodrow Wilson their third child and eldest son Thomas Woodrow Wilson." Fate could hardly have seemed more propitious towards a happy, good and uneventful life than it seemed at the christening of this child. Generations of religious, intelligent, sweet-tempered, normal people went to his make-up. His cradle was in a pleasant home where there was neither poverty nor riches. Self-esteeming, and much esteemed in the little community in which they lived, the Wilsons nevertheless did not seem of the stuff to set the world afire. From such a soil a spark of genius would not have been looked for; it was soil, however, to give sanity to genius. Wilson's reactions to life were always normal. Intense, ahead of his age, with high ideals, he nevertheless was practical and constructive.

Among the many tales told of a well-known head of one of the women's colleges in America is that when announcing the death of a poet she said, "Hereafter I shall announce the birth as well as the death of a great man." Most biographers make such announcements, but they have to prove their case.

Woodrow Wilson was the most famous man in the world in 1918. Was he a great man? Throughout the entire world his name is known, but he himself is unknown, so paradoxical, so conflicting are the accounts given of him; and this in spite of the fact that the man is exposed with every sentence he writes. Pick up a letter of his, leave off the address and signature, leave out any identifying facts, and no one familiar with his style could possibly mistake it as coming from any one else. Furthermore, had any member of his family seen a letter written to him, he would have been able, before seeing the answer, to know what that answer would be. But around all political figures looms the myth and the caricature. With Woodrow Wilson they assumed fantastic proportions. The myth began with his birth: he was said to be a Virginian. It would be just as true to say that Lincoln was a Frenchman if through some chance he had happened to be born in Paris. There is some legal quibble about a country's claiming the birthright of any one born in its dominions, but there is no mistaking the species. Wilson left Virginia when he was a year old. And that, with scarce a year's law course at the University of Virginia in 1879–1880, is all the contact he had with that State. He believed in the myth, and Virginia also believed in it, which is sufficient to show what the man thought of the State and the State of the man.

His ancestry on all sides had taken root in Ohio soil; he was the product of the Middle West. Nevertheless the myth persists; it is useless to argue against it. One chronicle after another waves its facts aside, ignores Ohio and places him in Virginia. He is called a Virginia president and he himself liked the title. When all is said we come nearer to the truth when we consider him as non-sectional. Something of the simple constructive attitude of the pioneer always remained with him — the Western breed; but his youth was spent in the South and the emotional romanticism, always strong in him, was no doubt helped on by the Southern environment. The Scotch strain was evident in his moral attitude. Intellectually he steps out of his inheritance and is just himself — the great pacific statesman obsessed by a cause for which he was to live in ever widening circles.

II
BOYHOOD AND STUDENT DAYS

Strange creatures lie in ambush to beckon the growing boy. He, who is undeflected, has seen a star that is his, knows a straight path, and takes it.

Chapter Two

BOYHOOD AND STUDENT DAYS

IN 1858 Joseph Wilson left Staunton to take charge of the First Presbyterian Church in Augusta, Georgia, a sleepy Southern town of 16,000 inhabitants. His family consisted of his wife, two daughters and his infant son Woodrow. All Joseph Wilson's earlier life, with the exception of his two years at Staunton, had been spent in the Middle West, and he had the traditions and mental outlook of that part of the United States. His wife's experience of America had also been almost entirely Western. But a clergyman quickly identifies himself with a community and Joseph Wilson was soon a conspicuous figure in Augusta, where he and his family lived through the fateful period of 1861 to 1865. The quarrel between the North and South came to a head when, in 1861, Sumter was fired upon. At once war was on between the sections. The seeds of trouble had been sown in the very earliest settlement of America. There could be no light comradeship between Cavalier and Puritan, and even more than the social difference was the economic difference. The South was agricultural, the North commercial — these were the fundamental causes of irritation. Men like Lee and Lincoln were powerless in the end against the storm of prejudice and hate that swept through the country.

Woodrow Wilson was four years old when Lincoln was elected and eight when Lee surrendered. His memories of these days were necessarily very dim. Augusta was out of the line of battle and the daily lives of the Wilson family were not fundamentally touched by the national tragedy. Joseph Wilson sympathized with the South; more than that, he identified himself with it, but he was not of the blood. He could look compassionately upon troubles around him without a personal sense of bitterness. His finances were not greatly affected. The big church and comfortable manse stood for order and, no doubt, to his son they represented the height of beneficent power where he could be safe and happy in the midst of any outside turmoil. His life was as simple and uneventful in outside diversions as a boy's life could be. The school he attended after the war was taught by an ex-Confederate officer, a man of culture, and his boy companions were rather a fine set. A few remained his friends to the end of his life.

The records of his school years, handed down by eyewitnesses and relatives, are not impressive. It is unfortunate for those interested in his early life that he was rarely given to reminiscence. He was always so eagerly bent on what concerned him at the moment that, to make him recall the past, was like trying to divert a river from its course. One legend of his boyhood is certainly untrue, that he did not learn to read until he was eleven because mentally he was rather slow. He would have been a dull boy indeed if he had taken to books and rules of thumb instead of listening to his father's impassioned interpretations of life. It would seem that he was physically lazy, which may be due to the fact that he was not robust; but beyond doubt mentally he was amazingly alert. The temper of his mind was early manifested in his passion for making rules and constitutions, organizing clubs and assuming leadership among his boy companions in the executive side of their lives.

In spite of the excellent results of this boy's upbringing, it would not be safe to suggest it as a model for most boys. He was given his own way in every particular and lived in an atmosphere of adoring admiration. Fortunately the admiration was mutual. If the father called the boy's mind "gem-like," he, on his part, thought his father's mind "God-like." To the ears of today it sounds rather excessive, but it was the language of that period and especially of that section of the country; and the devotion between father and son was as genuine in fact as it was sentimental in language. The father saw in his son his own ambitions and ability; and to these he thought was added genius. He steadily inspired him with his own confidence, assuring him that he was born for leadership. He also insisted on his thinking out his ideas logically and speaking them clearly in well-constructed phrases. They enjoyed playing with phrases and words as others enjoy playing a game. Later, in one of his rare reminiscent moments, recalling these days to the writer, Woodrow Wilson said, "I was swollen with pride as I listened to my father's preaching; and if he hesitated for a word I would, in my mind, supply it. I can still feel that exultant thrill of joy if I got the right word in my mind before he voiced it from the pulpit. I look back over my boyhood and think of the evenings when we gathered together to read Dickens. Can you imagine old or young weeping or laughing over any of the writers of today, and an entire community watching for the next instalment of their work?"

The Reverend Joseph Wilson was considered an eloquent preacher; he had as great a love of the spoken as of the written word. The dogmas of the preachers of those times were drawn from a bedrock of convictions, and woe unto the person who tried to refute them! Christianity had to show its passport through the portals of a theological church, not the Church through the portals of Christianity. Though of all the churches the Scotch Presbyterian was the most rigid. Woodrow Wilson's boyhood was spent in no uncertain atmosphere as to right and wrong, and always his own personal responsibility was pressed upon him.

The absorbing study of the household was that of the Bible; the Old Testament stories were always on his father's lips, and the leadership that he urged upon his son was really that of the Old Testament heroes, an omnipotent God behind their adventures, and their efforts for a cause, not for themselves. Once the boy remarked to his father how dreadful it was that Moses, the leader, should not have reached the promised land. His father's answer was, " It was God's will and his work was done."

The boy was sustained on all sides by influences that kept the course of his life undeflected, uninterrupted. Consequently he was never a child in the ordinary sense; even his humour was mature; it was somewhat on the order of that of the preacher or politician, whose anecdotes and stories delighted him. The usual boy's humour, which is to see something standing on its head rather than on its feet, anything distorted out of its proper perspective, a boy's irresistible love of a practical joke so excruciatingly funny to him, so exhausting to his elders, he never enjoyed. It is difficult to imagine what he would have liked in his Christmas stocking; one does not associate toys with him. The picture of him comes before us, perched in the big pew in his father's church, his tiny legs not reaching the floor, his eyes in great spectacles fixed with rapt attention upon his imposing father as he boomed away in the pulpit. All the time he was solemnly checking up on the sermon, and any mistakes were registered for future discussion. The child's home life was perhaps too soft, perhaps too superior, and there were no outside diversions; but he escaped being a prig by the simplicity of his nature and the warmth of his heart, and by the fact that both he and his father could laugh at themselves when their logic failed. We see a very old-fashioned child, one Miss Edgeworth would have skilfully depicted, and his illustrious end would have been happily portrayed by her, only she would have attributed it to morals rather than to brains.

In 1870 when Wilson was fourteen his father accepted a professorship in the Theological Seminary at Columbia, South Carolina; and at the same time he was made pastor of the First Presbyterian Church in that town. Sherman's army had wrecked almost everything in Columbia except the Capitol building and a few of the churches. The poverty-stricken people were slowly putting roofs over their heads and trying to adjust themselves to new conditions. The salaries from church and seminary, though meagre, made of Joseph Wilson a comparatively well-to-do man in Columbia. His wife, moreover, received a legacy at that time and they built what seemed to the people about them a luxurious home. So Woodrow Wilson's boyhood continued in an environment essentially similar to that of Augusta — his people the most prominent, and his house the most comfortable in the community.

The school he attended was held in a barn opposite his house and the master was a man of culture left destitute by the war. It was a far better school than the majority of boys can find today, in its poverty of equipment and its directness of intellectual purpose. The goal was definite and the path to it straight. Nevertheless he was not keen about standardized studies; his mind was working with his father's along lines congenial to them both. Theology and politics fought for precedence in this home; with the boy politics was well in the lead. The entire South was given over to these two subjects. The Theological Seminary was a building constructed out of an old stable, but eminent preachers from all over the South came there and prayed and preached. It is a curious picture brought before us — this group of men arguing about intricate theological problems in the midst of very practical needs and bitter suffering, to which they were by no means indifferent. We are sure young Woodrow Wilson was not concerned with the elaborate frame the theologians wrought about Christianity. He no doubt saw that the men were bigger than their theories, and he thought their prayers wonderfully eloquent. As a matter of fact he then and always took his religion very simply. His father and the Presbyterian Church must be unquestionably right; having accepted these premises he dismissed theology from his mind and enjoyed his Bible, his God and his prayers without the least struggle with his intellect. This was by no means the case with his political studies; they absorbed every moment he could spare. It was a portrait of Gladstone, not one of the Fathers of the Church, that as a youth he hung over his desk.

Hopes that they will be leaders are common to ambitious youths; they need no outside suggestion. But what was uncommon in this youth was his early maturity, his singleness of purpose and his moral robustness. At sixteen he was starting to study the charts of the great explorers in political history, and unconsciously fitting himself to sail the ship of state. To call this egotism is absurd. When a man feels he has a gift for painting he studies, not to be a sign painter, but a master. This is true of every line of life, and young Wilson was only working to fulfil his destiny. He looked back on the years spent in Columbia with more pleasure than on any other period of his life — just why it is not easy to understand, for from all accounts of his early life, youth seems to have passed him by. The aphorism that a man should live through his ages may have much to be said for it, but if a boy can happily and naturally absorb the wisdom of age and escape the follies of youth he gets a big start in the race of life.

When he was sixteen years old Wilson went to Davidson College, North Carolina; at the same time his father left Columbia and moved to Wilmington, North Carolina, to take up a pastorate in that city. This first experience of undergraduate life at Davidson College in the seventies determined his attitude when he became President of Princeton, for he saw what some men could do on very little and what they would have done if only they had had a fair chance. He was not a poor struggling boy when he went up to College; but the College was very poor and everywhere around him were men who longed for opportunity. Never after that experience could he look even tolerantly upon effortless youth who needed to be coaxed to take advantage of what he and his friends considered the highest privilege in the world, the opportunity to get wisdom. From that time on one of the prevailing motives of his life was to bring about fair play, the democracy of opportunity. After only a year at Davidson his health broke down and he went home to recuperate. For the sake of truth one illusion must be destroyed; the so-called "curious illnesses," to which he was subject from time to time, were of a most unheroic character — nothing more or less than acute indigestion, and very easily explained.

Before the Civil War the dining tables of Southerners literally groaned with every edible water or land could produce, transformed into delectable creations by the famous old black cooks, blazing hot rolls with golden butter, buckwheat cakes and molasses, fried chicken and pound cake — a food epic might be written about them. With such delights exercise was imperative, and in antebellum times the Southerners lived largely out of doors, fishing, hunting, riding. Much of their time was spent on horseback; a horse was to a Southerner what a gondola is to a Venetian. After the war, however, the horses gone but the black cook still on the job, the results were disastrous. All through his life Wilson suffered from the Southern idea of a meal, combined with little exercise of the body and intense exercise of the mind.

During the years at Columbia and Davidson the aftermath of the war was about him. He saw the bleeding pride of the South, the fearful wreckage of beauty and tradition. All this not only sank deep into his heart, but it was intelligently, almost dispassionately considered; and his reasoning about it led to his life's convictions. War was not only a vicious act towards humanity, it was an act that shamed reason. Given that war become inevitable, then at least the nations should have the sportsmanship of a prizefighter and not kick the fallen foe. Peace should come without victory. Over and over again he said these words, but the conviction was brought about in his youth. He knew that a foe that is ruthlessly crushed is always revenged. Every ruthless victory is a Pyrrhic victory. He heard of the splendid gesture of Grant to Lee but he saw what followed — the reconstruction days and the carpet-baggers, the maggots that devoured a weakened civilization after the monstrous folly of war. The ideas conceived in these early days were those he worked over all his life. Had Wilson been the son of Southern people it might not have been possible to keep his judgment unprejudiced. He often said, "The only place in the country, the only place in the world, where nothing has to be explained to me, is the South." That was true, but it was true because he was impersonal as well as personal. From his unclouded comprehension of the North and of the South he gained much of his broad knowledge of the essentials in the life of the nation.

One of the most arresting incidents in Wilson's life — he was only nineteen — was when he said that he thought it unfortunate to have a Decoration Day for the graves of the Southern dead, as it sustained a national bitterness. Every emotion of his heart was in sympathy with the stricken people about him, but his friends were antagonized. They were in no mood for tolerance; their wounds were too raw.

The world of the aristocratic South was over; at the moment of its defeat it became an historical field for poets, for romanticists and novelists, a land for the exploitation of carpet-baggers. Wilson's mind was turning to the future and to the reunion of the sections. Ten years earlier a far different man, Robert E. Lee, had urged upon the people about him the same ideas: "Forget the past; remember only that you are citizens of the Union." But Lee belonged to the past. He worked for the sake of others and for the future; but he himself could never be a living part of it. Wilson was young; the past was, for him, only history. He saw the onward sweep of democracy, and himself a part of it, perhaps a leader. To leave the atmosphere of Lee for that of Wilson is like passing out of the dim light of an ancient cathedral into the bright light of a workaday world — the old going out and the new coming in.

Before the Civil War the College of New Jersey at

Princeton had been the favourite educational institution for Southern boys; many men who became leaders in the South had been educated there. For some years after the war few Southern boys were sent to Princeton, but later it regained its popularity with that section of the country.

After his almost cloistered social life for nineteen years in the South, Woodrow Wilson approached the outside world through the little antechamber of this college. The awkward boy of nineteen was a very mature man in mind and character, but his experience of life was limited to a few Southern towns. Many men have immaturity with experience; it is very rare indeed to find maturity with inexperience. The conditions of his early life placed him in the latter group.

For the first time he was thrown with people from other parts of the country. His companions, mostly from the North, with the enthusiasms and prejudices of youth, were violently upholding the point of view of the Civil War dominant in their homes. Coming directly from a region suffering from the war and from the miseries of reconstruction, he refused to argue its rights and wrongs with boys who had no realization of its horrors and consequences. He would debate a principle with any one seeking the truth, but he would not argue futilely with any one who merely wanted to indulge a prejudice. Such an attitude made for peace and respect; and even in his freshman year he won a commanding place by his convincing sincerity of purpose, which was always joined to courtesy of manner.

The group of young men who formed his most intimate friends was a very pleasant one, with more brains and morals than is generally credited to the undergraduate. They were religious as boys go and perfectly harmless, so they naturally called themselves " The Gang " and their club " The Alligators." To Woodrow Wilson it was the first taste of carefree youth, and it did not go to his head but it did to his heart. His comradeship with his classmates was unusually intimate; and with a few, a very warm and permanent friendship was formed. In every crisis of his life the Class of 1879 supported him.

The light-hearted atmosphere reacted upon him; it is said that he actually danced a hornpipe! Perhaps he did. There was a fresh bumptiousness about the Princeton undergraduate that would have been equal to involving the Pope in such a pastime. Wilson liked to believe he enjoyed this life, it was so young and free and gay, and youth and freedom and gaiety the circumstance of his life had, for a time, submerged — and so he longed for them. It was altogether to the good that this serious-minded boy from a broken world could listen sympathetically for a moment or two to a lighter note. He stood intellectually apart, his training and purpose quite different from those of the boys about him. Weak in the classics and the standard college curriculum, he was saturated with the knowledge of the English statesmen and English politics, and he could have produced from memory an amazing amount of theology.

Dr. McCosh (President of the College from 1868 to 1888) had abolished the secret societies and established two literary societies, the Whig and the Clio. Wilson joined the Whig and soon became the acknowledged leader in all its debates. But debate with him was not a mere play of wit; it was pre-eminently the means of arriving at the truth, and he was never willing to support a side that was not in harmony with his convictions. As he later said, in speaking of John Bright, " To the orator this atmosphere of sincerity and honest conviction is a mighty power." On one occasion a debate had been arranged on the tariff, and to his Club, the Whig, had been assigned the defence. He was unanimously elected to represent his society, but he absolutely refused, although he would have gained much honour for the society and much distinction for himself. Great indeed must have been the force of his personality to be able to keep the love and friendship of his companions when they unquestionably thought that he should add to the glory of their society rather than be so nice about his personal opinions. But in a later debate in which he argued against a protective tariff he scored a great success.

He was made speaker of the Whig Society and was considered its best debater. There was no muddling of thought when he spoke and he was quite determined there should be no muddling of speech. Oratory was of the utmost importance to him as by means of it he could make his arguments effective with an audience. His youthful efforts in that direction must have been trying to any one not on fire with the subject. He told a story of how, when home for his vacations, he would go into his father's church when it was vacant and, standing in the pulpit, would try his voice out addressing the distant empty seats. One day he noticed that the negroes he chanced to meet in the town were particularly obsequious, bowing to him with exaggerated politeness. He was greatly puzzled until some member of his family discovered that a negro passing the church had peeped in and seen him apparently addressing the spirits, and negroes don't miss their manners or trifle with anything queer like that. He laughed when he told the story, then added with a perplexed frown, "I'm Southern, but I have very little ease with coloured people or they with me. Why is it? For I care enormously about them." The answer might have been that they were always children and he had never been a child. At this he would have been indignant and would have said that his had been a beautiful childhood — so it had been — and that he loved children — so he did — but nevertheless the answer would have been a true one.

At Princeton he organized a Liberal Debating Club among his classmates, writing out its constitution after the manner of the British system of parliamentary government. Questions for debate were introduced by the Prime Minister and unless he was able to support his policies his side went out and was succeeded by the opposition — an exciting game which he originated and in which he played a leading rôle. It was perhaps unfortunate that during his undergraduate days he had little outside stimulus to scholarship, but as what knowledge he gained came in great part from his own efforts it increased intellectual self-confidence. The way he used the college library was a revelation to his classmates.

Convinced that all progress depended upon leadership, he concentrated his studies upon the lives and works of great statesmen, especially the English. Everything he did was directed to help forward his life's purpose. During his sophomore year he published a sketch of Bismarck, and the following year one on Chatham. In these he showed a remarkable insight into the different problems confronting the English and the Continental politicians. The English statesman must persuade his people by debate and oratory; the Prussian statesman had only to convince his king; he was independent of political parties.

His most important essay during his undergraduate time was that on *Cabinet Government in the United States*, written in his senior year (1879).

The politics of the country were at a very low ebb. For twenty years the government had been in the control of one party which dominated by force in the South and held the North and West in line by appealing to the passions aroused by the Civil War, "waving the bloody shirt," as it was called. There were no important issues between the two great parties; the elections were mainly a scramble for office. Some eminent writers ascribed this condition to universal suffrage. But Wilson did not concur. By a careful analysis and comparison with the English parliamentary system, he showed that the root of the evil lay in our legislative system. He pointed out that legislation by Congress was really in the hands of irresponsible committees and was rushed through with little or no consideration by the Congress as a whole — a system that failed to develop leaders because it gave no scope for leadership. "Eight words contain the sum of the present degradation of our political parties: *No leaders, no principles: no principles, no parties.*" Congress passed laws but had no part in their administration; the President and his Cabinet administered the laws but had no hand in their enactment. The Convention of 1787, in its desire to make the executive, legislative and judicial powers of the government independent, "made their separation so complete as to be isolation."

With the optimism of youth he suggested, as a remedy, that Cabinet officers be selected from representatives of the dominant party in the House, and have seats in that body with the right to initiate and to debate any proposed legislation. "They would constitute a link between the legislative and executive branches of the general government;" and would lead to a responsible ministry. "Government by irresponsible Standing Committees can bear no comparison with government by a responsible ministry."

He believed that public debate was the means of securing a responsible government. "Debate is the essential function of a popular body." It serves two purposes: it subjects a proposed law to a close examination and it educates public opinion.

The essay is so full of thought and searching analysis that it deserves to be read in its entirety by students of political science. Although written when Wilson was only twenty-three years old, it remained his political *credo* to the end of his life.

The effect of his experience at college was exhilarating. The influence he gained over his comrades and the favourable notice in the outside world of his essay on *Cabinet Government* confirmed him in his belief that he was equal to taking an active part in the political life of his country; but he was poor and without influence as well. Yet Lincoln had been in much worse circumstances. What he thought of Lincoln, and he had a habit of thinking of him all through his life, had a tonic effect. In later years, referring to this period, he said, "When I remembered Lincoln and thought of all my greater material advantages, and the same longings and hopes and fears for my country, I thought I would be a poor creature indeed if, even without genius, I was not able to do some constructive work for the land that bore me and that I so loved."

The path towards his goal seemed logically the law; and after his graduation at college he went to the University of Virginia and entered the law school there in the autumn.

Situated near the foot of the Blue Ridge Mountains, the University of Virginia, built in beauty and surrounded by beauty, has a quality of reserve and tradition unusual in the United States. It represents in form and spirit the personality of its founder and architect, Thomas Jefferson, who, as Wilson said, was " an aristocrat by nature and a democrat on principle."

About the University lingered the atmosphere of the old South. The graves of the Confederate dead, the home of Jefferson at Monticello, every line of the beautiful old buildings, silently, irrevocably kept faith with the Confederacy. Wilson was in deeper waters of conservatism than he had ever been before, and he loved the place, but he was uninfluenced in thought. A Federalist on principle, he believed that the uniting of all sections of his country should take precedence over all other matters, which explains why a sympathetic attitude towards Jefferson was not evidenced until later in his life. Yet, in spite of the strongly Southern atmosphere of the conservative community in which he was living, he quickly became popular with his colleagues.

The reputation he brought with him for scholarship and skill in debate and oratory increased. No longer a boy, his lack of boyish gaiety was not missed, while his quick wit and humour were appreciated. At last his years had caught up to his maturity. The standardized law courses were necessarily endured, but his interests kept their habitual course in the line of American and British politics and political leaders.

During his first year at the University he joined the Jefferson Debating Society, was elected its president and, true to his custom, revised its constitution. It was before the Jefferson Society that he gave his oration on John Bright. With amazing courage and intellectual honesty, he explained John Bright's attitude towards the Southern Confederation, and his own. He said:

" But I am conscious that there is one point at which Mr. Bright may seem to you to stand in need of defence.

He was from the very first a resolute opponent of the cause of the Southern Confederacy. Will you think that I am undertaking an invidious task, if I endeavour to justify him in that opposition? I yield to no one precedence in love for the South. But *because* I love the South, I rejoice in the failure of the Confederacy. Suppose that Secession had been accomplished! Conceive of this union as divided into two separate and independent sovereignties! To the seaports of her Northern neighbour the Southern Confederacy could have offered no equals; with her industries she could have supplied no parallel. The perpetuation of slavery would, beyond question, have wrecked our agricultural and commercial interests, at the same time that it supplied a fruitful source of irritation abroad and agitation within. We cannot conceal from ourselves the fact that slavery was enervating our Southern society and exhausting to Southern energies. We cannot conceal from ourselves the fact that the Northern Union would have continued stronger than we, and always ready to use her strength to compass our destruction. With this double certainty, then, of *weakness* and *danger*, our future would have been more than dark — it would have been inevitably and overwhelmingly disastrous. Even the damnable cruelty and folly of reconstruction was to be preferred to helpless independence. All this I can see at the same time that I recognize and pay loving tribute to the virtues of the leaders of Secession, to the purity of their purposes, to the righteousness of their cause which they thought they were promoting — and to the immortal courage of the soldiers of the Confederacy." (From *Public Papers.*)

This incident shows two distinct sides to his personality. He was almost weakly sensitive to praise or blame and to a sympathetic and affectionate personal atmosphere; on the other hand, he was entirely and coldly objective when an intellectual problem was under consideration. Perhaps that is why his friends so loved him and why his political enemies so detested him.

He took part in many other debates, and wrote an essay on Gladstone; altogether it was a year of great mental activity. He formed lasting friendships, and always amidst his friends there was one closest of all. When a boy in Columbia it was young Brooke; later, when he was nineteen at Davidson, it was John D. Bellamy. At Princeton his devotion was more equally distributed among his classmates, but Robert Bridges had a little the lead. Now, at the University of Virginia, it was Heath Dabney. The surprising thing is that friendships beginning with such intensity were never relinquished.

It was very unfortunate that he could not remain long enough at the University to take a degree in law, but at the end of the year his health broke down and he was obliged to return to his home, where he spent a year and a half slowly recovering his strength. During this time he continued his studies in law and politics, working as he liked, independently. He taught his little brother Latin and straightened out his father's papers; and it is recorded that his mother said, "It is sad to have Woodrow not fit; but it is such a joy to have him in the house." Rather a big achievement for a highstrung, temperamental, ambitious young man, the wind out of his sails, in dull waters, and suffering from an indisposition that is ranked high for bringing on a state of devastating depression.

In the spring of 1882, feeling once more in good form, he decided to go to Atlanta, Georgia, and open an office there, with the expectation of starting a law practice that would enable him to plead principles of law before the courts — the entering wedge for a career in public life. From his outlook he had good reasons for these expectations. His essay on *Cabinet Government in the United States* had brought him into prominence; he was a skilled debater and orator, and he must have realized that he had a more fundamental grasp of the principles of law and the science of government than the men with whom he came in contact. But he had not recognized the low intellectual level to which the South had sunk as the result of the reconstruction processes. Atlanta was not a university town; it was a small city which was looked upon as the coming commercial city of the South; and young men flocked there with the hope of making their fortunes.

He formed a law partnership with Edward Ireland Renick, who had been a fellow student at the University of Virginia. Their ideals and purposes were much the same and a close friendship between them began at once. They selected their office, put it in order and waited for clients. None came. Into this office one morning entered young Walter Hines Page, filling it with his gay laughter, his bright friendliness, and the political gossip of the land. A Tariff Commission, appointed by Congress, was holding hearings throughout the country and was now at Atlanta. Page, representing the *New York World*, was traveling with the Commission, having a delightful time making it look ridiculous. Wilson and he and Renick agreed on every point and grew eloquent over their determination to fight the protective tariff. Page was greatly impressed by Wilson's familiarity with the subject and urged him to go before the Commission and represent the public — show these fellows up who were only speaking for small selfish interests. After much urging he agreed and made an address before the Commission. He used arguments suitable to the British House of Commons. His friends declared his address was great; a few men of education in the town congratulated him on his insight into the subject; even he himself was a little impressed, especially as he had not lost his temper when the Commissioners jeered at him. But if he had felt they were beneath contempt, they, on their side, thought him a young ass, and were convinced his talk would merely bore the crowd and do no real harm to the protective tariff. They yawned in his learned young face.

He was not disheartened; he called together a few of his friends, Page among them, and organized a branch of the Free Trade Club of New York.

Page and Wilson met for the first time in Atlanta and neither ever forgot the impression each made on the other. They had the same conception of, and outstanding attitude to, right and wrong; their political outlook was the same, as Page's letters reveal. It was unfortunate — for Wilson especially — that their paths diverged, for Wilson always greatly needed the fresh air and sunshine that a nature such as Page's brought.

In October of this year Wilson took his examinations for the bar; and in March he qualified for the Federal Courts. He visited the local courts and saw lawyers, with some reputation for ability, vigorously prosecuting or defending for a small fee some ignorant negro accused of a misdemeanour or petty crime. The State legislators were ignorant and indifferent; they saw no further than their own personal advantage; the good of the State was of little concern to them. When the question of meeting the cost of the public schools was under discussion they looked for help to the Federal Government. Wilson was disgusted. He thought the State should be independent, should stand on its own feet and attend to its own internal affairs. But no one cared what he thought.

He and Renick sat in their almost clientless office and sadly realized that they had made a mistake. It was the first blow that had come to him, and it was a bitter one. In his heretofore sheltered life he had been flattered by every one who had come his way; and he had reason to feel that he had power — he knew that he had — and that it lay in one direction: the political arena was his field. He felt himself equal to putting up a big fight for his principles, but the path that seemed the most direct to his objective was blocked! Well, he would find another, but where? He would have none of the low crowds he had seen in the Atlanta courts. He had been living in imagination with statesmen, and that was the company he intended to keep. American political government should yet be better because of him! But how? All these heartburning questions and young highflown aspirations were discussed with his father, and the two agreed that he must go back to his studies and find his opportunity in the academic world. Many notable Englishmen had found their way to politics from university positions. The Johns Hopkins University was offering great opportunities for advanced work; it might be well for him to go there, continue his studies; and then, no one knew what might happen! His father's robust optimism and absolute faith gave him confidence to decide on this plan.

In the spring, before leaving Atlanta, he met Ellen Axson, and the one-time Commissioners would entirely have understood every emotion he expressed in his notes to her. No pedantry now! He was as unsophisticated and romantic as all the world feels a young man should be. He had been fortunate so far in his friendships, and now in his love he was supremely so. All women who held his attention he endowed with some qualities of his mother.

Ellen Axson might have been his mother's daughter. His estimate of her was a true one. She was lovely to look upon, with a grave sweetness of nature and a cultivated taste, and she was utterly unworldly. Her material desires were as small as those of her young lover, and she shared with him a very serious outlook towards life's responsibilities. There could never be any clashing of ideals in the lives of these two. She was the daughter of a Presbyterian minister, living in Rome, Georgia, and the traditions of their lives were much the same.

The courtship was an extremely rapid one for those days; five months after the first meeting they became engaged (September, 1883). When she spoke to her brother of her engagement she said, "Woodrow is the greatest man in the world." This conviction steadily strengthened as the years went by. As neither had any means their marriage had to wait until he should finish his studies at the Johns Hopkins University and somewhere secure a position that would assure them an income.

When, in 1883, Woodrow Wilson entered the Johns Hopkins University for post-graduate study in history and politics, it was an auspicious move on his part. The Hopkins offered just what he wanted. He had applied for a scholarship but, for some reason, his application was turned down. It is quite possible that his education was too desultory; and his reputation for oratory and debate would not have helped him much at the Hopkins.

It was at this period of his life that I first appraisingly saw Woodrow Wilson. He had often visited Baltimore during his undergraduate days at Princeton, and our families were friends. But it was on this occasion, as I remember it, that his personality impressed itself on me.

At an evening reception, crowded with Baltimore's

smartest and least academic set, I was talking with a group of immaculately dressed youths when I noticed, entering the room and making his bow to the receiving party, a tall young man with a formal, oversensitive manner. "Look at Woodrow Wilson," said one of the group about me. "Now how does he manage that bed-side manner and make his dress clothes look like a preacher's? He's terribly clever but he's provincial." And I recall, as I still critically watched him, answering, "If he's provincial he's making the provinces look bigger than the city. He has personality; he is distinctly the personage in this room." At that moment he turned and caught my eye and came smilingly towards us. He joined us with a self-conscious diffidence which invariably overtook him at a first approach, but quickly passed away once the ice was broken. He said, rather apologetically, "It's so delightful to see a few people whom I know. One feels so lonely in a function like this, so very much a stranger. I wonder why we have such functions — but that is ungracious." "Now Woodrow," said the youth who had called him provincial, "don't be a Hopkins genius. We are fed up with them here in Baltimore. But how do you like the Hopkins?" He hesitated and said that it lacked the atmosphere of general culture which is found at the University of Virginia, but that it was doing splendid scientific research and was a wonderful place in its way. "Unfortunately," he added, "I like my own way too much for my own and other people's comfort." Then turning to me he said, "Don't you think we might find some place out of this crush where we can really talk?" We found some chairs against the wall and talked chiefly of his work and his ambitions, of the government of the United States and of his satisfaction over the inauguration of Grover Cleveland as President. And he made a swift, running appraisement of our Presidents from Washington on to Cleveland. He spoke whimsically of his appearance, which he felt was unfortunate for one who wanted to go into political life. "Now, no man," he said to me, "would, on account of my Scotch physiognomy, ever familiarly slap me on the back in a hail-fellow-well-met way." "How would you feel if they did?" I asked. He laughed delightedly as he answered, "I should just hate it; I should be most uncomfortable; I could not conceivably slap him back, and what a prig I should feel because I couldn't. But now I think of it, no one would slap Grover Cleveland on the back, and yet no one could think of him other than a man of the people. It's unquestionably the cut of my face; it's too bad." It was a remarkable face, I thought, strong and heavily marked, naïvely young but full of power. It must have been drawn, one might think, for the caricature of a Scotch covenanter and then transformed by an idealistic inner light that obliterated everything that might have been ugly.

There was a diffident graciousness in his manner and in the quality of his voice that marked him as coming from the South; but the moment the talk touched on the problems of the country all diffidence and youth were lost, and he led the conversation with vivid brilliancy. He had a characteristic way of throwing back his head, apparently seeing something far off, not dreamily, but very distinctly, and then coming back to the general talk with some little whimsical word.

The discussion turned upon America and its leaders, and his admiration and reverence for Lincoln was arresting in a young Southerner. "You seem to place Lincoln in your heart above Washington and Lee," I said. "In my heart, yes," he answered. "Washington, Lee, Lincoln! " he exclaimed, his eyes shining with enthusiasm. "Such contrasting personalities! You can't compare them; they were only alike in their integrity and greatness. Washington gave America her liberty; Lincoln's gift was the heart." He might have been a college undergraduate championing his boy heroes. I recall laughing at his spread-eagleism and saying: "And yet, after reading what you have written, I think, with all your love for America, you should have been born in England." To which he indignantly replied, "Would you pigeon-hole a man as an alien because he imports some of his fuel from outside? A man should be able to look upon life as a whole and without prejudice. I think there are few things so poor and cheap as prejudice — and so pernicious."

His eagerness for a political career seemed strange to me, and his disregard of prejudices not an asset towards its success. It seemed to me then as it seems to me now that he was made for an English statesman and not for an American politician.

The vivid impression he made upon me that evening not only has remained unchanged, but it has become accentuated. As I meet him in memory down the long years, I see him, as it were, like a developing negative that has grown clearer and more definite as time went on. The habit of escaping from a crowd for just talk was characteristic of him. His absorption in essentials, his wit, his humour and his seriousness, all were placed before me that evening of long ago. Deeply in love, as he was, with the girl he was engaged to, I felt, as he talked of her, not so much his romance as how greatly he loved her, and I realized that to come within the circle of his friendship would bring one into a genuine atmosphere.

Old Baltimoreans did not appreciate the line the Johns Hopkins University was taking. They would have much preferred an ordinary college of the prevalent American type. They were deeply rooted in tradition. Good manners, good living and culture, these were theirs by inheritance and the grace of God, and efficiency was not greatly appreciated. If gifts were to be dispensed in their community they belonged first by right to their own people. President Gilman of the Hopkins ignored local talent; he scoured the world for men of genius, or men who, he thought, would develop genius, for the heads of his different departments. To the Baltimoreans many of his selections merely looked queer; and if they were geniuses then genius should be avoided. It caused great offence to some of Woodrow Wilson's Southern friends that he was not given a post at the Hopkins. One afternoon we were taking tea at the house of a friend when a number of his admirers surrounded him and dramatically voiced their opinion that he should have the best post at the University, minimizing their compliment by stating their low opinion of that institution. For a moment he looked embarrassed; then a humourous twinkle came into his eye as he took up the defence of the University and its President. President Gilman had an uncanny eye for the right man, he told us. If he should elect him now to an important post, his modesty would be ruined for life. "I should pat myself on the head and say, 'He thinks me a genius, and consequently I must be one.' It would be my utter ruin; Ellen would refuse to marry me — she puts the virtue of humility first among all the virtues."

It was all jestingly said, but as he walked home with me he referred to it again, saying how absurd it all was when he had not yet won a starting place in the world. And I remember that he went on to speak of his deep faith in Democracy and his conviction that the old order — the dear Baltimore people we had been talking to — was passing away. I thought as I listened that what would be to them the end of all that makes life worth while, would be to him the beginning. It was the day of violent individualism and he, with his accentuated individuality, was giving all his hopes and thoughts to what would benefit the masses; he was far ahead of his age. He made for me an unforgettable picture of a man apart.

The Historical Department at the Hopkins was under Herbert B. Adams, a distinguished historian, who had been trained in Germany and who was especially insistent on collecting accurate facts regarding local history and institutions. He had started a series of monographs called the *Johns Hopkins University Studies in History and Politics*, which was absorbing the attention of the Department when Wilson came to Baltimore. It was not the order of historical research that appealed to him; and he did not contribute to the series. Once he impatiently remarked, "Facts, facts, facts! What do I care about his facts? What I want to know is what he does with them." Wilson himself lived with his facts, seeking their explanation as he went along. The hard work he did, and he was a tremendously hard worker, never gave the least impression of drudgery; it was always vitally alive.

In his essay, *Mere Literature*, written many years later, he expressed his ideas of how history should be written. "In narrating history you are speaking of what was done by men; in discussing laws you are seeking to show what courses of action and what manner of dealing with one another men have adopted. You can neither tell the story nor conceive the law till you know how the men you speak of regarded themselves and one another. I know of no way of learning this but by reading the stories they have told of themselves, the songs they have sung, the heroic adventures they have applauded. I must know what, if anything, they revered; I must hear their sneers and gibes; must learn in what accents they spoke love within the family circle; with what grace they obeyed their superiors in station; how they conceived it possible to live, and wise to die; how they esteemed property, and what they deemed privilege; when they kept holiday and why; when they were prone to resist oppression, and wherefore — I must see things with their eyes, before I can comprehend their law books. Their jural relations are not independent of their way of living, and their way of thinking is the mirror of their way of living."

Adams, recognizing the ability of his rebellious pupil and believing in his power for independent research, relieved him of routine work and encouraged him to follow his own bent. It was to Adams' credit that he could act with such justice, for the two men were antipathetic — Wilson, largely self-trained, with the English and Scotch inheritance of strong individualism; Adams imbued, as has been said, with the German system. Dr. Adams once said to me, "When I look at your friend Wilson, I feel as a trainer might feel about a promising horse. He may back him even though he may feel a little dubious when he sees the quiver of his nostril or the toss of his head. There is something a little over-intense about that young man from the South. Is he solid? Will he be able to see that there are more ways than one to Rome? Has he the temperament to endure strain?" There was no doubt of Adams' lack of intensity nor of his possession of solidity and also no doubt that he was a remarkable teacher. The seminar, conducted by him, was a source of delight and profit to Wilson. There the professors, instructors and graduate students met weekly about a long table and freely discussed questions related to their studies in a general atmosphere of comradeship and equality. It was here that Wilson met and formed a valued friendship with Frederick Jackson Turner, who later became distinguished as a historian. He always attributed to Turner the recognition of the influence of the frontier on American history and politics, a conception which has thrown much light upon American character and on the development of American institutions.

The English statesmen and the English system of parliamentary government had absorbed his attention from the time he was a school boy in Columbia. Walter Bagehot early became his model. When he first became acquainted with his political writings we do not know, but there can be little doubt that they fired his imagination at an early date and that they appealed to a kindred nature. From Bagehot he got the principles of responsible government, of the necessity for leadership, of the education of the people by public debate, of the importance of intimate relations between the executive and the legislative branches of the government. Bagehot's influence is evident in Wilson's article on *Cabinet Government in the United States*. The theme of that essay was developed further in his *Committee or Cabinet Government*, an article begun in Atlanta and finished soon after he came to Baltimore. Published in January, 1884, it received great applause from his companions of the historical department, and made such an impression on the staff of the University that he was awarded a fellowship for the following year (1884–1885).

This article was scarcely off his hands before he began work on what was one of the most important publications of his life, a book on *Congressional Government;* it was completed by the autumn of 1884, and was brought out the following January. The book was modeled after Bagehot's *English Constitution* and discussed the government of the United States as Bagehot had that of England. He refused to regard the Constitution as a fixed and rigid rule controlling the government in detail; he showed that it changed and grew under interpretation, as the country expanded and the habits of the people changed, and how the changes were necessary in order to make the Constitution work under new conditions. He traced the development of irresponsible committee legislation to lack of responsible leadership, the pressure of governmental business and the extreme separation of the legislative and executive branches of the government. He distinguished between the way the framers of the Constitution expected it to work and the way it works in actual practice. All this was done with such keen insight and philosophical understanding that he was immediately brought into great prominence as a writer on the science of government. Many editions of his book have been published and its influence is still felt.

The Johns Hopkins was almost entirely given over to scientific research, and Wilson cared nothing for any science except that of government, and that chiefly from a humanitarian standpoint. Yet with his approach to life so different from that of the men about him, and his manner and address such as to make the scientists suspicious of his solidity, he won a lasting place at the University, and a few close friends in the community. The years at the Hopkins were all to the good, but what he got from the University was determined by what he brought to it.

One evening he entered my drawing-room with a peculiarly buoyant air. His *Congressional Government* had made a tremendous success; University positions were being offered to him; he was to give a series of lectures at the Johns Hopkins; and there was no doubt he could be married in the summer. Sitting by my side, he said, in high spirits, " The world is a wonderful place; I can be married. My salary from my Johns Hopkins lectureship will bring me $500 a year, enough for my marriage and a few months afterwards; then, affluence! for $1500 will be added, as I have accepted the position of Associate in History at Bryn Mawr, a new college for women that is to be an intellectual spur to the female sex but masculine in its curriculum and devoid of all gentle weaknesses."

" Tell me something of Ellen Axson," I asked.

" Why, you know, of course," he said, " that she is the most beautiful woman in the world."

" That we will take as a matter of course. But will she interfere with your work? Will she try to make you over into something else? "

" Ellen would never interfere with any man's way," he replied.

" Not if he were going the wrong way? "

" In that case," he laughed, " she would be tactfully persuasive, not coercive. She is receptive, not aggressive. A man could read her a treatise or a long essay and she would never interrupt until the very end. She has, what I call, a speaking silence."

It was lilac time and the room was filled with bowls of those lovely flowers, the air full of their fragrance. It all seemed staged to send a sentimental young man joyously on his way.

He and Ellen Axson were married in June and took up their life at Bryn Mawr in the autumn of 1885.

III
AN INGLORIOUS DEFEAT

“ *Male and Female Created He them.*”

Chapter Three

AN INGLORIOUS DEFEAT

THE fact that he wanted to marry and have a home of his own obscured what, at any other time, Wilson would have seen — that he would not enjoy teaching " the new woman." His ideal woman was essentially a feminine one who, as he had said of Ellen Axson, was persuasive rather than coercive. The Dean of Bryn Mawr was certainly not persuasive. She had grasped in her masterful hand what she thought the soft boneless stuff of her sex. She would put it through a stiffening process and turn out an organism, not like a man, but something more effective — something like herself. In opposition to the general attitude of the women of that time she had very little reverence for the male as male. There was no word in the English language for which she had a greater disgust than sentimentality; it had been the bane of her existence in her early life and the age reeked with it. Her Victorian elders had dared to attempt to addle her fine brain with this stuff, but she had been strong enough to eschew it. To her there was only one dependable thing in the world — a good mind; and nothing brought it up standing but a good education. This she intended, not to offer, but to force upon her sex. President Gilman's clear-cut conception of education she took as her own — a high standard of requirement from the students and brains that could work, with authority to direct them. That she had one of the first requisites of an executive, the power of selection, was later evident; the professors she chose for starting her adventure all made excellent records in a big world. We must give this dauntless, able woman the admiration Wilson never could give her.

Dauntless and able himself, he was not overimpressed with the corresponding qualities in others and he thought they should exist without ruthlessness. Speaking of that unpleasant characteristic, he once said, " There is no sense of justice in a ruthless person; justice cannot exist without mercy and love; and justice is the supreme safeguard of civilization." If the Dean of Bryn Mawr had not possessed something flat-footed in her mind, and a very thick skin indeed, she could never have smashed her way, as she did, through every obstacle. She had no foes within herself but she had many foes without, whom she met with courage, brains and force. Woodrow Wilson would have suffered less, when he too fought with courage, brains and force for an unpopular cause, if he had been less sensitive.

Bryn Mawr was opened in 1885. On the platform at the inauguration ceremony were, as her big cards, James Russell Lowell and President Gilman. There must have been a twinkle in Lowell's humourous eyes; only in poems or in squibs would he venture on the woman question. President Gilman's ideal of woman was not militant, but he was always very courteous and hopeful. And young Wilson — there he was, steeped in romance, having his most cherished convictions scoffed at, and his reverent protective attitude towards woman looked upon by the militant ladies about him as too unintelligent for words. He would have been more fretted than he was in this alien atmosphere if he had not been able, when college duties were over, to escape to his own private rooms where the feminine question was settled to his entire satisfaction. His Southern wife could hold to old traditions with a will quite as inflexible as the Dean's.

Before leaving the Hopkins, Wilson had not thought it worth while to devote any time to taking the degree of Doctor of Philosophy. Now he was in the midst of a group of women who were fighting for intellectual recognition. Their one convincing card was a degree; it was to them a sacred and vital goal; they would not have credited an Einstein with brains unless sponsored by university examiners. The importance of Wilson obtaining this honour was urged upon him by the Dean, his wife joining with her in this matter. This surprised him until she explained, " I know your genius; every one does who has any sense at all, but so few have; and a silly intellectual badge may be a passport to a good position quicker than any other sign for people who cannot see below the surface. Then, too, I can't stand these women forever saying to me, ' Oh, your husband hasn't a doctor's degree, has he? So strange. Miss M— has one.' Miss M—! Such a limited little creature — and so plain." Wilson laughed delightedly over this, yielded and took his doctor's degree at the Hopkins in the spring of 1886, offering the *Congressional Government* as his dissertation. He said to me, " I took all this pother to please Ellen, and," with a twinkle in his eye, " in order not to be looked down on by my class, which consists of one young woman who is as capable of understanding political science as I am of understanding dressmaking. I cannot let her snub me." I suggested that it was very well for him to say that, but in truth he was afraid of his chief. His reply does not bear repeating.

It is amusing to see how Wilson, the fighter, was subdued at Bryn Mawr. For the first and only time in his life he failed to make constitutions and by-laws and to assume leadership among his associates; he made no such attempt with the feminists.

His total income from all sources was $2,000. It was pitifully insufficient to support himself and his wife and, in the third year of his stay at Bryn Mawr, two babies and two relatives. One of these relatives naïvely remarked that Cousin Woodrow was not exactly a domestic man, for he couldn't use tools. But he took care of the furnace and pumped water into the tank. Just why he should be damned as a domestic man because he couldn't use tools we don't know. One thing we do know: he took all the tasks as a matter of course; and perhaps in such ways made up in part for that deplorable lack of outdoor exercise which so affected his digestion.

His immense confidence in himself intellectually is frankly revealed in a letter written at this time (1886) to Dr. Hiram Woods, the death of whose young brother called from him an overflow of emotional sympathy for his friend — and for himself. The following extract is extraordinarily characteristic:

"Hiram, I have — as I hope you have not discovered, but as you doubtless have — an intellectual self-confidence, possibly out of all proportion to my intellectual strength, which has made me feel that in matters in which I have qualified myself to speak I could never be any man's follower. You will understand, therefore, how great must have been my admiration for Allan when I tell you that he formed in my thought the only possible exception. I have sometimes thought that when Allan came to the maturity of his powers I could, if not follow him, at least heed him as I would no other. If this reveals my overweening confidence in myself, it at least redeems that by showing how I could love and admire Allan."

Such confidence in himself might at this time seem merely youth's bravado, but it was part of the essence of his nature — the quality which made people so often exclaim, " Do you never think yourself wrong? " And the answer would always be the same, " Not in matters where I have qualified myself to speak."

His work went on steadily — as good work as he had ever done. His lectures were prepared with meticulous care. He wrote his essay on *Responsible Government under the Constitution*, an essay on the study of politics published in the *Princeton Review* in 1887; and the *Study of Administration*, published in the *Political Science Quarterly* the same year. He planned what he hoped would be a great book, a *Novum Organum* of politics. As a first step towards this he began a textbook to be called *The State*, in which he would describe the governments of all countries. This he intended to use, not only as a textbook for his classes, but also as a notebook for his greater undertaking. " A big task, especially in view of the condensation and clearness necessary for a book expected to be small enough and plain enough to be used as a college textbook; but a task full of profit and pleasure for me, and thoroughly well worth doing; because our language, so far as I know, affords no such work."

A great desire came over him to have done with teaching undergraduate girls, to go to Germany and come in personal contact with the great German scholars. It was a quickly passing dream; his wife was ill, another baby was on the way, it was difficult to meet even small coal bills. And when sorrow as well as trouble stormed at his door in the death of his mother he was very near the breaking point. The cold-blooded biographer wonders whether the ruthless Dean of Bryn Mawr had not some truth on her side when, as reported, she said that no one has a right to put a strangle hold upon one's work with such things as wives and babies — although I believe she said " husbands and babies." Whatever an outsider might think, this was not his thought. He was as incurably romantic about his wife and home as he was ambitious for his career. Go together they must; and, to his singular good fortune, his wife and family always saw with his eye and thought as he thought.

The many letters written by him to his wife and father during the years of his early manhood show an intensely emotional nature where his heart was concerned. His father's generation was a sentimental one; and in manner and in many of his convictions Wilson often seemed to belong to that age rather than to his own. In his personal letters he used his father's redundant vocabulary; it had become so ingrained a habit that often his words seemed a smoke-screen obscuring the unsentimental strength of his character, though they did not mislead those who knew him. In his political writings, his essays and addresses, the personal element dropped.

Many of his biographers use that great word " vision " in such a way that they destroy all its value and leave the impression that he was visionary. Nothing could be less in character. He had a goal, a very definite goal, which he saw before him, ideally right for humanity, practical and realizable. He spent his life attempting to reach it. In his heart he voiced the words of St. Paul, " Let us lay aside every weight . . . and let us run with patience the race that is set before us."

The word " lonely " has also been applied to him to the confusion of the truth. The truly lonely man is usually companionless. Wilson knew that he was incapable of enduring loneliness, and he never attempted to endure it for any length of time. Why it should be esteemed a virtue to be lonely is curious; it is really a great misfortune, and generally indicates a man's failure sympathetically to understand his fellow men. Only a very few times in all history do we see entire human comprehension and utter loneliness lifted to the height of great tragedy. Only once did Wilson stand beside the tragic figures of history—when, defeated, he handed over the reins of government to a party which was bent on throwing into the scrap heap all the policies for which he had given his life. He was, in the main, even more than most of us, dependent upon confidential friendship. He gave to his friends the warmest love, and it was returned to him in full measure.

One evening, in the spring of 1888, I was sitting over the fire in my drawing-room. I looked up to see Woodrow Wilson coming in, his face aglow. I had worried a good deal over the Bryn Mawr situation. I knew well his desire for leadership, a desire that seemed to have been born with him. I knew how he longed to make just laws for the decent common people, the vast mass of average men and women he understood (he understood no other class); I knew too that he believed his voice was their voice, and I realized how in these slowly moving years all that he said had seemed to him unheeded, echoless. Drawing his chair up to the fire he said joyously, "I am leaving Bryn Mawr. I have accepted the professorship of history at Wesleyan College, Middletown. My salary will be much larger; and moreover, I shall teach men."

The pleasant atmosphere that he brought about when among friends could partly be accounted for by the quick way he threw aside a disagreeable subject, turned all eyes with his to a bright outlook. He was leaving Bryn Mawr;

he was dropping a worrying pack from his shoulders, but his thought was at once transferred to his coming post and its opportunities for work. Humorously he touched upon his past difficulties. " The higher education of women," he said, " is certain to come in America whatever I think on the subject. And why not? It's just none of my affair now." Then he went on to talk vividly of his plans for the future. He visualized the people into something better than they were, ignoring the inertia of the masses. But when he spoke of the laws that must make his ideals at all practicable he was on solid ground. " We must get rid of the politician," he said, " and develop the statesman; we must have leaders whom the people trust and who are worthy of their trust."

As he talked all seemed very possible; the air about him was vital. Listening and looking at him that evening in the leisurely atmosphere of the fireside I realized afresh his extraordinary powers of inspiration. It was the day of such very small things for him, socially and professionally. It had always been that. Now he was about to take this post in a little New England college with the spirit of high adventure — and while he spoke glowingly of his new opportunities, of his hopes and aspirations, I seemed to be standing at an open window looking out on a reconstructed world where there were happy homes, thrifty farms, simple, unsophisticated schools, and everywhere the spires of little churches.

His was the pioneer's attitude, not the hunter's, and I wondered whether the peaceful, unadventurous goal he planned for the average man would be satisfying to any except one far above or below the average. But his belief that he knew the people remained undisturbed, and, like his religion, it was not open to argument.

The years at Bryn Mawr had done much to destroy what was, at best, a late youth. He did good intellectual work there, but it was done under a disquieting strain, for a duller existence than he lived at that time would be hard to imagine. The whole episode must be looked upon as a detour from the main course of his life.

In the autumn of 1888 he and his family went to Wesleyan. It had some of the characteristics of a small college in an English university in its close touch between the students, who numbered only two hundred and eighteen, and the faculty. His two years there were as peaceful as any in his life and full of intellectual achievement. He formed, at the start, strong friendships with members of the faculty. They accepted his leadership and he entered with a rush of energy into the college life. With an increase of salary, congenial companionship and men to teach, he buoyantly picked up that part of himself which had, apparently, been suppressed for three years under the thumb of the Dean of Bryn Mawr. There is something ridiculously boyish about it. He wrote constitutions and instituted reforms — was himself again, a leader. He took careful note of the effect of his lectures and addresses, not only for the good of his classes, but because the reactions of undergraduates might serve as a gauge of his ability to hold a larger audience. He was painstaking and industrious in every task. One can account for the immense patience of this very impatient man, who hated boredom with a passion, only by recognizing that he had inherited from his ancestors a very steady-going machine that would register accurately no matter how rapidly he drove the engine.

His biographers have emphasized four sharp turning points in his career: his religious awakening when he united with the Presbyterian Church at sixteen; his emotional awakening when he met Ellen Axson; his intellectual awakening when he went, an undergraduate, to Princeton; and at Wesleyan, his political awakening. He, too, thought this an interesting point of view; he was fond of using the phrase (he did love a good phrase) "when a man comes to himself." But nothing could be more absurd where he was concerned. His feet, when he began to walk, were set straight on the path he took, the only unusual point being that he never diverged. He joined the Church at sixteen as naturally as a stream follows its channel. Every trait in his ancestry led him naturally to respond to the type of Ellen Axson when, to his good fortune, she came his way. He brought to Princeton, as an undergraduate, an intellectuality that startled his easy-going classmates; and at Wesleyan he only advanced further in the political studies begun at his father's knee. No! There were no turning points in his career. But in addition to all the inherited qualities that could be absolutely counted on, there was still his own personality.

It is a truism that a great man is never typical; he either develops old ideas and makes them live, or he starts a new idea and gives it life. Wilson's entire undeviating purpose was to make alive the idea of a sound democracy; and his effort was to bring that about through improvements in the methods of government. Little Wesleyan was a laboratory in which he worked untiringly. There he finished his book, *The State*, long thought out and carefully worked over; and there too he wrote a pregnant essay for *The Atlantic* on *The Character of Democracy in the United States*, from which a few sentences may be quoted: "Our democracy, plainly, was not a body of doctrine; it was a stage of development." "Such a government as ours is a form of conduct, and its only stable foundation is character." "Monarchies may be made, but democracies grow."

Always his standpoint was that of a great teacher of the underlying principles of life. He was a firm believer in the power of oratory, and the caricatures of him in that line always amused him. It was said of a famous divine, who could hold a congregation spell-bound, that after a powerful sermon on the Beauty of Love and Peace, his reaction from it was so great that he would make his own home unbearable for the rest of the day; after which he would be entirely relieved and be ready for a sermon on Sweetness and Light in the evening. The popular orator or preacher or pedagogue has his temptations, but they were not Wilson's. His words were the outcome of a life recklessly given for his principles; he lived as he asked others to live.

It was during his Wesleyan days that he wrote a notable review of Bryce's *American Commonwealth*, with eager appreciation of that important work. He only adds here and there a criticism where he, as an American, sees from the inside what Bryce, as an Englishman on the outside, fails to see. These small differences are not derogatory; they merely throw an additional light on the road he is taking with the writer *con amore*. He differs from Bryce in thinking that American methods of nomination are essential to democracy; and suggests two serious weaknesses in our election machinery: the multiplicity of elective offices, and the requirement that a candidate be a resident of the district which nominates him.

Of all men with whom Wilson came in contact Bryce most nearly resembles him in mental outlook. Had their lives been thrown together they would not have struck any sharp corners of difference, nor have felt they must hold in reserve something the other would fail to understand. Consequently Wilson's review of *The American Commonwealth* is a critical analysis of his own thoughts.

From a student's point of view things seemed to be going very well with him, but when the offer of the chair of Jurisprudence at Princeton came he moved on, little knowing that his great contemplated work on politics was doomed and that the door was being opened leading, though still far off, to an active political life. The migration from one small college to another larger and more influential would seem but the natural continuance of a scholarly and uneventful existence. It was, in reality, the beginning of the end of his life as a scholar.

IV
THE PRINCETON PROFESSOR

“ *A man imprisoned in a task.*”

Chapter Four

THE PRINCETON PROFESSOR

WILSON was thirty-four when he took the chair of Jurisprudence at Princeton — a very quiet prelude those thirty-four years, from which he emerged with his only assets in his brain. He had obtained a wider recognition for scholarship than he realized; and it was enhanced by that elusive quality, of which he was entirely unconscious — personality. The intensive study of his one mental absorption, political science, made him, as President Gilman of the Johns Hopkins University said a few years later, "a master of the principles which underlie a free government."

At first the atmosphere of Princeton refreshed him; there were interesting men in the faculty and they were warmly appreciative of his ability and sensitive to his charm; the students were enthusiastic and he had crowded classrooms. His teaching was of the order of the popular preacher who inspires his people and leaves the result to God and their conscience, an attitude that was most satisfactory to the ordinary undergraduate, whose conscience did not trouble him and to whom God's judgments were more distant than those of his Dean. In reality Wilson had no muddled thought about teaching; the delight of the undergraduate over his lectures did not deceive him; he knew that inspiration should be followed up. Even at this early date he had in mind the tutorial system.

Princeton, under the presidency of Dr. Patton, was far from satisfactory to progressive men. Many of the faculty were dissatisfied and keen for reform. Wilson united with this group and became its leader. No one could have been more desirous than he to get, not applause, but results. Princeton was the hotbed, or bulwark of theology, as you please; but the theologians had not succeeded in instilling other-worldliness into the undergraduates. The youths of Princeton were filled with many burning desires neither intellectual nor spiritual. There was a quality about them that would have deterred a less dominant fighter than Wilson from attempting to impress such material with his convictions of what a college should be. " The object of the University is singly and entirely intellectual," he wrote. How could any one so delightful mean anything so crude as that, the boys thought; but he was so humorous, perhaps it was a joke. The faculty, however, knew he meant what he said, and believed he would carry it through. Though the younger members of the faculty were heart and soul with him, some of their older colleagues felt he was going too fast and might become difficult. Why not let well enough alone? If there was one strongest desire among the students it was for social success, and this factor in the complex problem Wilson could not at all comprehend. To desire something social for any other reason than that it gave you pleasure was a point of view undreamed of in his philosophy. A snob was out of his horizon; and, as the world is full of snobs, this limitation of comprehension was a dangerous rock ahead for him.

As always, his home was an oasis. When he opened its door he was in an atmosphere of entire sympathy with all his ideals and ambitions, and of an almost adoring love; it was a household without conflicts. For this he was himself largely responsible. Many men, doing the work he was doing, and which he felt, given the opportunity, he could do greatly, would have been irritable over the lack of money and the many small economies that pressed upon him and his wife, but he put the happiness of his home circle before everything else; that was his choice — his own greatest pleasure. Any one who has been the guest of a man who is worrying over addresses and epoch-making writing, who is following out a train of thought and torturing his brain for the right word, knows that his host is apt to be temperamental and to resent interruptions. Selflessness is very rare. In Wilson's pleasant home the guests had never to consider the moods of the master; for somehow they found him ahead of them in considering theirs. It was here you saw vividly the sweetness of his nature. His daughter, Mrs. Sayre, said to me, " As children we never opened the door to the room where he was, even when he was engaged in important business, that his quick glance toward us was not one of pleasure. We saw that he was occupied and we might not interrupt, but his looks said, 'You can't come in now, but the glimpse of you is delightful.' We never had an impatient word from him, no matter how well deserved."

His Princeton home always meant more to him than any other place. After one of his visits to Baltimore he reached Princeton in a blinding storm, and wrote of the desolation that met him when he reached home. The letter is dated February 25, 1902.

> " I reached home without adventure, notwithstanding the wreckage the storm had wrought all along the route. My train was only some fifteen minutes behind hand at the end of the journey, though the telegraph wires were down and it was running without the usual signals. — When I reached home I found that my apprehensions had been well-founded. My dear father

was in the midst of one of his attacks. It is over with now, and he is as well as usual; but I feel much safer at his side. — The scene of desolation that met me here when I got back was quite indescribable. Princeton is almost stripped of its glory. Its real glory was its trees; and the weight of ice piled upon them by the fine rain and chill airs of the storm stripped and tore them as if some malicious giant had studiously broken every branch away upon which their dignity and grace and symmetry depended, — and done it with a vicious wrench at that, so that the wound might be as deep and ragged and lasting as possible. Our own little place has suffered so much that it is fairly heart-breaking, — I have had the blues deep in me ever since I saw it first in the dim, beclouded, dismal moonlight of Saturday night! One or two of our finest, stateliest trees are now mere scarecrows, and much of what we most loved about the place is gone, — and Ellen and I are worshippers of trees, — chose this spot for the splendid fellows who are gone! "

And as he warms to his subject he quotes that lovely poem of Lanier's, *A Ballad of Trees and the Master:*

> Into the woods my Master went,
> Clean forspent, forspent.
> Into the woods my Master came,
> Forspent with love and shame.
> But the olives they were not blind to Him,
> The little gray leaves were kind to Him;
> The thorn-tree had a mind to Him
> When into the woods He came.

. . . . .

In spite of his appreciation of this poem, which he felt was his personal possession, he himself would never have sought consolation in the solitude of nature. Unquestionably, under dire circumstances he would seek shelter in the hearts of the people who loved him, or, in a commonplace way he would go to church, preferably to a Presbyterian church. There was nothing of the mystic about Woodrow Wilson; he had no love of solitude; his final reactions were always simple and human. In this letter of the trees, after voicing his sorrow over their destruction, he ends on his usual note, that he was happy none the less in his dear home, and that his chief delight in his visit to Baltimore had not been in the acclaim given his address or in the announcement of his degree, but in being with the people he loved. It was the simplicity of his social life and his personal tastes that bewildered many who watched his spectacular official life. To one who understood this every thing he did fell into place.

During the early years of his Princeton professorship his vitality was at its strongest and his life more varied than it had ever been before, although it was still socially in a very limited and sheltered atmosphere. It was said by many that he was the most popular professor Princeton had ever known. He made quick personal contacts, and, as was his habit, among his group of close friends there was one closest of all: John Grier Hibben learnt his every thought and ambition. Wilson must see him daily; he must see him many times daily; before an idea had time to materialize or inspiration to cool his friend must hear it. Mrs. Wilson's generosity to her husband's friends had become proverbial. If any man or woman cared for him then they were certain of her affection. There was a good deal of the maternal in her attitude towards her own generation, while to older people she had always a filial attitude. These years of Wilson's expanding friendships found her wholly sympathetic. "I have talked with Jack Hibben," he would say, "and

I am refreshed." Her instant smile showed her gratitude to the unseen Jack Hibben. Or, " I am writing Mrs. ——; she does help you when you are feeling sluggish." And her answer would be, " She is a true friend; one never feels that way about a person unless she is rare and true." But if any one disliked her husband she felt it almost too astounding to be contemplated. He, or she, must, wretched creature, be entirely depraved or hopelessly dull. On the other hand, if Wilson took a quiet prejudice against some one she sought to disabuse him.

Contrary to the usual impression, he had few intimate friends among women; nearly all his intimate friends were men. His friendships were more like those among Englishmen than among Americans. A gathering of his friends would usually be in quiet home surroundings, and good talk would be their recreation. His appreciation of an affection given him was out of the ordinary as was his need of personal love. A person, to obtain his intimacy, had to say very definitely, " I like you," or " I love you." After that, if you were sincere, your life became his personal and unfailing concern.

To make one's friends appreciate each other is not an easy matter. His letters of introduction for one of his women friends almost always began, " You will feel her charm at a glance." Of a man he would write, " You will at once realize his fine nature, his powers of right thinking." The recipient of one of these notes often saw none of those charms and was very bored; and the idealized often found it trying to live up to unfamiliar virtues. It was especially trying when he introduced in glowing phrases two women and each thought the other too awful for words, but dared not say so. I think no one would have been brave enough to criticize one of his friends to him.

With his intense interest in the personality of a friend, and his entire confidence in a quick characterization, which he never failed to make, it is curious how little he did know about any one who was at all subtle. He had a model for men and women, made out of his own traditions, which at first sight he fitted to any one he felt drawn to. Many things, such as a recognized place in the sun, a big bank account, personal vanity, he was so indifferent to that they hardly registered in his consciousness. Consequently, he passed over with closed eyes many other things, trivial to him, that help to make or mar the person. If disillusion came he bore, with disconcerting patience, the small faults he had not at first seen, and kept his eyes, as much as possible, on the virtues he had seen. Once he had made a close friend loyalty literally took possession of him and he would not let go. One thing was incumbent — the friendship must be mutual. His personal friends each held a place with him entirely apart from all others; he could not conceivedly be confidential about one friend to another. Any of them might easily believe that he was closest of all. Certainly he would know without question that his place would never be taken by another, exactly as he would know that at a moment's call Wilson would be at his side.

He was apt to theorize about friendship, quite unconscious that he himself was simpler than his theories. In one of his theorizing moods he wrote me:

"Sometimes I am a bit ashamed of myself when I think of how few friends I have amidst a host of acquaintances. Plenty of people offer me their friendship; but, partly because I am reserved and shy, and partly I am fastidious and have a narrow uncatholic taste in friends, I reject the offer in almost every case; and then am dismayed to look about and see how few persons in the world stand near me and know me as I am — in such wise that they can give me sympathy and close support of heart. Perhaps it is because when I give at all I want to give my whole heart, and feel that so few want it all, or would return measure for measure. Am I wrong, do you think, in that feeling? And can one so deeply covetous of friendship and close affection as I am afford to act on such a feeling? "

As a matter of fact no man has many friends who come up to this standard; and as he had a few who did he was richer and not poorer than most men. It was a pity that he could not enjoy a number of friendly acquaintances, usually good enough friends — men who would give him recreation, yet not trouble his or their hearts overmuch; but he couldn't; so his life was at once richer and poorer.

Robert Bridges, in his *Testament of Beauty*, states accurately what Wilson expected when he found a friend:

> " What a man looketh for in his friend and findeth,
> . . . .
> is his own better self, his live lovable idea,
> flowering by expansion in the lives of his life."

We, his friends, dearly as we knew he loved us, were quite sure he would not have known whether our eyes were blue or brown; but our ideas, our lives, he knew — or thought that he did; were they not a living part of his own? Invariably when he spoke with ardour of a friend it was his charm of character that he emphasized, his own ideals " flowering " in them.

With his intense nature one would suppose that he would have been a bitter adversary; but he seldom bore a grudge. " What a detestable person! " That was usually the end of it. He denounced and forgot in a breath; no carrying a stone up his sleeve or hounding a fellow creature! He was too absorbed in great issues to be petty; and his thoughts were wholly given to measuring up to what a man should be who desired to serve his country.

There were three classes of people for whom he had no attraction: The general run of women, the party politicians and the self-indulgent class, poor or rich. Pretty young girls were not attracted to him nor he to them. A fast woman bored him as much as he bored her; party politicians were enraged by him; and the self-interested avoided him.

In all his letters and notes at this time he was just a little afraid that he might be thought egotistical; he had a sneaking fear in his heart that he was taking himself too seriously, and that hurt his sense of humour. But how could he fail to take himself seriously when everyone about him, from the time he could walk, had taken him seriously? Those who knew him only through his letters and writings thought that he lacked humour, but in conversation, or when addressing an audience, he was witty and quick at repartee, with biting sarcasm for an opponent and a queer whimsical humour for a friend.

More and more convinced that his chance for a voice in the affairs of government must come through his writings, he became obsessed about his style. It fretted and worried him. He approached the ornamentation of literature with the seriousness that he approached the structure. Smart writing, a pose, or sentimentality, were insufferable to him; truth was essential everywhere, but the words and sentences in which one conveyed that truth must be effective enough to reach the multitude — it was all very worrying! To write an essay and not have it read would be sad — wouldn't do at all, etc., etc. It was " enough to make a wise man scratch his head and think." So, a few days after our conversation, he sent me his book of essays, *Mere Literature*, begging that his style of writing be criticized with ungloved hands. My answer to this letter was a disavowal of critical ability and an expression of my pleasure in the essays, which brought from him his own estimate of what he had written:

PRINCETON, 18 June, 1897

". . . I must straightway prove my right to call myself a critic by pointing out to you two cardinal defects in what I write. There is, first, a serious structural defect, noticeable most of all in the literary essays, but to be found also elsewhere, — for example, in the "Washington," particularly in the earlier parts. The transitions are managed *too* smoothly: the several stages of the argument are not distinct enough: you bring away no definite outline, but only a recollection of certain passages and a general impression of the whole meaning. The treatment plays in circles; it does not move with directness along a clear course.

There is, besides a fault of style: and here, again, the literary essays are the best field of observation. The phrasing is too elaborate: has not the easy pace of simplicity. The sentences are too obviously wrought out with a nice workmanship. They do not sound as if they had come spontaneously, but as if they had been waited for, — perhaps waited for anxiously. The fact is not so. They come fast and hot enough usually, and seem natural moulds for my thought. But I am speaking of the impression they make when read, — the impression they make upon *me* after they are cold, — when read in the proof, for example. I write in sentences rather than in words: they are formed *whole* in my mind before they begin to be put upon the paper, usually, — and no doubt that is the reason they seem *cast*, rather than naturally poured forth, and have lines of artificiality in their make-up. — I might carry the criticism into other points, — but these will, I trust, sufficiently illustrate my critical capacity! I feel bound, once and again, to study my work objectively.

You must have been conscious of these defects, architectonic and of detail, but were too generous to speak of them. Then, too, it is my serious business to study my own art, particularly as I have a big piece of work in hand in which such faults are apt to be telling — a history of the Country from the settlement till 1889, written with an attempt to let the story tell itself, as nearly as possible without commentary by the historian, and keep the atmosphere and illusion of each age as it passes. Alas, that I should have set up an impossible ideal in "The Truth of the Matter?"

In a way your generous appreciation stimulates me as much as your critical analysis of what I have *not* done might have instructed me. Knowing you, I know how much it means that you should take, not the critical, but the sympathetic attitude when I write or talk for you. It must mean that you find me at any rate genuine; and it heartens me as it should that you so believe in me. A man who wishes to make himself *by utterance* a force in the world must, — with as little love as possible, apply critical tests to himself; and the best critical tests, surely, are the standards of those he can trust to see and utter the truth about the art he practices.

It is not likely I shall be in Baltimore another winter. The Hopkins' losses have made it necessary to cut off all lectures not essential to instruction, and, though they were willing, I believe, to renew their engagement with me, I did not see my way clear to allow it.

By admitting a general, mixed audience to my lectures, they had made it impossible to preserve their original character as class lectures; and by allowing them to *count* as class lectures they made it impossible for me to make them really popular. They were unable to enter into any new arrangement, — and I find myself *reduced* to letter writing to preserve my hold on the dear friendships I have made in a place that has come to seem to me almost like a second home. This is one reason I am sending you a long epistle; — like a man afraid to be cut off. . . ."

In the autumn I received the following letter which conveys, as do all his notes, a determination to succeed, if not in the active life he wanted, then as a writer:

". . . Perhaps, if you think of it seriously, you are encouraging a vice in me by talking to me of the matters about which I ask your critical judgment! I sometimes fear that it is a mistake to think too much about the way in which the things I seek to do ought to be done. I hate to hear *other* fellows talk solemnly about their " art "; and I often feel foolish when I recall how very seriously I am taking myself. And yet, if I know my own heart, it is not myself, but my work that I study and would perfect! Take the matter I have in hand: it is impossible, if I would do worthily, not to study it critically as a question of art. I am about to begin a school history of the United States, partly as a preliminary sketch and study in proportions for the larger canvas upon which I am at work; partly in order that the southern schools may at least be offered a history written in the national spirit and yet thoroughly just, with the justice of sympathy, to the South's principles and point of view. And yet it would be folly to add to the almost numberless manuals of this kind another manual. It must be a work of art or nothing — and I must study the art. I must cultivate a new style for the new venture: a quick and perfectly pellucid narrative, as clear as the air and coloured with nothing but the sun, stopped in its current here and there, and yet almost imperceptibly, for the setting in of small pictures of men and manners, coloured variously, as life is. I have never yet done anything of the kind and I do not know that I can do it. Neither the style of the essays, nor the style of the Washington will do — and I have no other, except that of " Division and Reunion ", which is equally unsuitable — And thoughts of these things bring me back to your letter, with its delightful suggestion that ages, like days, have their own spirit and atmosphere, each bringing a peculiar message and demanding a peculiar response. Unquestionably it is so, and what the writing of history demands is that the historian give himself wholly and with entire resignation of his own crotchets, to the sympathetic rendering of these, being as careful to belong for a little to the age of which he writes as to know what its events were. Oh to be a seer and to have an imagination that would enable one to be of all ages a contemporary! — But tell me how a school history ought to be written, — and read with leniency my essay sent under another cover."

He showed how eager he was to make his words express himself when he wrote:

. . . It would be an invaluable thing to a literary fellow, seriously bent upon acquiring a real mastery in his art, to have abundant, various, and ever fresh material for studying that most elusive, and yet most central, question of the craft: how individuality is expressed.

It was characteristic of him to suggest to a friend, whose writing he thought effective, that they should write each other twice a week, each criticising the other's letters. Had a latter-day historian read such a correspondence he would have sensed a romance and have been brought sharply to earth when he discovered that the series was merely a literary exercise. This passion for perfection of style partially accounts for his voluminous correspondence. Yet there is another trait that helped to add to the huge store of letters: it was that no friend or friendly acquaintance ever wrote to him for sympathy, even about petty worries, that his response was not on the instant. No personal affairs, or affairs of state, delayed his reply to any call where his affections were in the least involved.

As one reads his letters one realizes the intensity of the strain he puts into his work—it must be perfected from every angle. For a moment, now and then, he wonders whether he is not too serious, but it is only for a moment. At once he takes up his quest for perfection and gives an ideal picture of how history should be written, as the work of a temperamental artist and of a coldly objective scholar. The reader should carry an impression of its outline and structure and yet get a boundless view of the play of life.

How tight the net of circumstance seemed to encompass him! Even in his writing he could never escape from his own watchful, overcritical eye, and all the time he was laboring to take his theories out of books and put them into action. At the bottom of his heart he knew he was free only in speech.

He was a very rapid thinker, and after some idea had become as clear to him as a mathematical formula, he took his recreation in tossing it about among a group of friends. There was gay badinage, but the trivial held him only as the lightest of surface comedies. He quickly cut through it to the great problems of the past, the present, the future. The unessential drew him hardly at all, but, because of his humour, and also because of a certain vitalizing quality that was his in a rare degree, he was never ponderous. He was subjective only inasmuch as he minded blame and cared for praise. For the rest he was purely objective. He was not often given to monologue; what another said was eagerly caught up, enlarged upon and enriched as he tossed the ball back. His friends felt that they had expressed something worth while, had given him some new impression; and his humour and wit in replying to them were unfailing except when a jest bordered on religion or sex. Then he became a little angular; one caught a glimpse of the rigid Presbyterian the caricaturists like to draw. The line, however, between theology and religion was very strongly drawn; the former was merely a habit, a tradition; it went no deeper than the form of his features. Religion was one of the deep joys of his life, so interwoven with the fibre of his being that the two were indistinguishable.

One evening his hostess was a very beautiful woman of an older generation, who had lately become blind. In the group over the coffee cups there were three or four Presbyterians. Some one said, "It is hard on you, Mrs.——, such an Episcopalian as you are, to listen politely to all these Presbyterian glorifications." She laughingly replied, "Why, I think the Presbyterian Church is a great church. How could it not be with such men in it as Mr. Wilson and —— and ——? The only thing I don't quite see is why you like it." This delighted Wilson, and always afterwards it was a byword with him: "I only don't see why you like it." As the laughter ceased and the talk went on about creeds and dogmas the maid came to lead Mrs. —— from the room. As she reached the drawing-room door she turned to wave " Good night "; and he, watching her, said, " What do our creeds and dogmas amount to? There goes incarnate religion! "

Some years later his hostess died. A number of his letters lie before me telling of the warmth of his love of one whom, though over seventy, he placed among the young dead. " The vastness of such souls as hers," he wrote, " makes time negligible." Later, when we were together, he dwelt much on his last talk with her, telling how he had said to her, " Give me the secret, for my work's sake, of the power you have with people. Why is it that everyone comes to you with all their joys and sorrows? Why do they tell you everything without hesitation? " And she had answered him laughingly, " People come to me because I am blind in more senses than one. I believe what they say, as they say it; and when they go I forget all they would have me forget. So nothing can ever be used against them — not even against their own self-esteem. The secret is that I know and love people, and do not expect too much of them. Why should I, knowing my own limitations? " Then he added, " She looked at me with those beautiful, blind, all-seeing eyes, and said, ' You, I think, too often try to put a gallon in a pint cup, and you choose too rich a vintage for the quality of the cup.' All she meant to infer," he continued, " remains in my mind. You see I must understand all kinds of people if I am to do the work I mean to do." How great that work was to be he did not faintly realize, but often when he failed the failure came from his belief that he understood people. He did not; he always idealized the quality and the capacity of those to whom he was giving the best he had. He was sure that he knew the masses when he only knew their needs, not their desires.

The uplifting, inspiring atmosphere he could bring was felt only when he was in a company of friends, or when he spoke to an audience, which he always visualized as an individual whom he saw in a perspective of friendly approval. When in the company of people alien in purpose to him, not his kind, he was either somewhat aloof in manner, a little difficult or a little diffident. Even in these early days his name was never mentioned that it did not bring about a conflict of positive opinions: the caricature, the myth and the man had even then taken distinct shape; he was a demagogue or a superman, or just an inspiring and very human man. Once the ice was broken and his shyness dispelled, the disagreement about him might remain, but there was never indifference; his figure remained in the foreground.

He used no gestures when he talked; his hands were always quiet; every emotion, however, showed in his eyes. Usually kind and quizzical, they became, in conversation, the gauge of every phase of the social atmosphere about him — coldly hostile to the pure scientist with whom he was not congenial, indignantly impatient to the purely intellectual, and glowing with warmth for the humanitarian.

One evening a motley group came unexpectedly together, among them Wilson and Albert Michelson, the distinguished physicist, and the two made a strong contrast. Neither could speak without calling forth from the other a hostile glance — Wilson with his conviction that behind everything was an invincible moral law; and Michelson, who thought less of morals than he should have and did not hesitate to say so. Great scientist though he was, there was something of the naughty school boy about him, and contact with moral idealists made him sulky. He stalked off to a corner of the room, seated himself on a divan, took a pencil and paper from his pocket and made sketches of the pious members of the group. The sketch of Wilson was so vicious that the hostess threw it quickly into the fire — which was really too bad. After Michelson had tossed the sketches to the company and gone away some one said, "I think we had the devil in our midst." To which Wilson replied, "No, no, the devil is not so clever, and he has manners. How I wish you had kept that sketch! To laugh at yourself has a tonic effect."

During the winter of 1895–1896 he overworked so that towards the close of the college term his health had seriously to be considered. His right hand became useless from what, at the time, was called neuritis. He therefore practised writing with his left hand; and his typewriter came into more steady use; later it served him even for his private letters.

After much urging he was induced to go abroad for a complete change. He went to England and Scotland and, for the first time, saw the parts of the old world that had held much of his thoughts all his life. His joy was almost pathetic, and he absorbed everywhere the things that entirely suited his nature. The beautiful Lake country was his own; he would have been a stranger in the vast forms of nature. Wordsworth was the poet he most loved and Grasmere was always his to return to in spirit. In the last days of his life he dwelt on William Watson's poem, "Wordsworth's Grave," and felt himself there:

> Afar though Nation be on Nation hurled,
> And life with toil and ancient pain depressed,

Here one may scarce believe the whole wide world
Is not at peace, and all man's heart at rest.

Rest! 'twas the gift *he* gave; and peace! the shade
He spread, for spirits fevered with the sun.
To him his bounties have come back — here laid
In rest, in peace, his labour nobly done.

It was a great boon given him for remembrance.

He made pilgrimages to the tombs of his political heroes, Burke and Bagehot. Dutifully he visited museums and art galleries, and attended a few concerts; but in antiques, painting or music his taste was very unsophisticated. Architecture was the one art he thoroughly understood — the beautiful man-made creations growing out of tradition and inspiration. The climax of his delight was reached at Oxford; there indeed he felt he had met his own. He was to carry with him from that enchanted spot some ideas of university administration that were to cause him trouble later on.

Every moment of his trip was of benefit to him. It was perhaps the first time in many years that he had been free from heavy responsibility. The muscles of his arm and hand relaxed, and he returned to Princeton in the autumn, seemingly well.

October 21, 1896, was a great day in the annals of Princeton, its sesqui-centennial anniversary; and its official name, The College of New Jersey, was then changed to Princeton University. Invitations had been sent broadcast to many notable personages. The appreciation Wilson had won in the college was shown by his being chosen to make the principal address. The title he chose was "Princeton in the Nation's Service." His oratory carried his audience, and the thought behind the words was quoted in many leading papers. It was Princeton's day and naturally she loomed overwhelmingly in the address; but read later — today — it is Wilson that stands out so distinctly, his ideals, himself. Though he had said, "The object of a university is simply and entirely intellectual," and though he had meant to force intellectuality upon his colleagues, one sees that he meant to force other things with it that he thought more important. "College professors," he said, "could easily forget that they were training citizens as well as directing pupils." His ideas apply distinctly to a college, not to a university — scholarship imperative, but training even more so; and religion the only possible atmosphere for life. It is the statesman who is speaking to us after these long years, not the college professor. His ideal of a college was undoubtedly a true one; the university, with its indifference to anything but perfection in some one line, might follow; but the college might make or mar the average man. His own life, however, followed the other plan; he specialized almost from boyhood. Fortunately, his specialty, the science of politics, was broad. He studied it as a living and progressive science, from history, literature, laws, customs and poems. He had written, "The science of politics is the science of the life of man in society" — a conception broad enough to make him an active influence in any place where he was stationed, though not broad enough to give him full comprehension of any specialty without a human interest.

The Princeton years brought to him a wider social experience; he was entering more and more into an active as well as a theoretical life. For the first time he traveled beyond the relatively narrow limits of the Eastern seaboard States. A lecture tour through the West which took him as far as Denver, made him realize that books and hearsay had not given him a thorough understanding of that region. Furthermore, he discovered he could hold audiences of any type. These lectures enhanced his reputation as an educator and public-spirited economist.

During his professorship at Princeton he wrote many articles for magazines on political, historical and educational subjects. He published two volumes of essays, *An Old Master* and *Mere Literature*, a *History of the American People*, a *Life of George Washington*, and, what is his most important contribution to history, a volume of the *Epoch Series* on *Division and Reunion* (1893), in which he discusses the causes leading to the Civil War and the conditions during the reconstruction period. His general argument is as follows: The Constitution was accepted without enthusiasm by the original thirteen States. They were all jealous of their sovereignty, and looked upon the Federal Government as their creature and not as their superior. It was the general belief that a State could withdraw from the Union if it so wished. This belief persisted in the South; but a national sentiment slowly developed in the East and West. The new Western States owed their statehood and therefore their allegiance to the Federal Government. In 1860 there were twenty States thus created which did not have the traditions of States' Rights still strongly held in the South. In reliance on these traditions the Southern States seceded from the Union in 1861. Wilson showed that they were within their legal rights, but that the growth of a national spirit in the rest of the country had practically annulled these rights; that the nation did not really exist as a nation until made so by the result of the Civil War. The war was to hold together a Union that had not existed before, and to make a Union for the future. This is a very valuable and important interpretation of the history of the country, and is accepted by historians generally. As Dodd sums it up: " The South was right in law and constitution, but wrong in history. The East, on the other hand, was wrong in law and constitution, but right in history."

In his correspondence with Professor Albert Bushnell Hart, the editor of the *Epoch Series*, he shows for the first and perhaps only time in his life that he recognizes that he is not wholly Virginian. In claiming to bring to his task an impartial outlook, he recalls that his father was born in Ohio, his mother in England, so that his point of view was not wholly Southern; moreover, in political philosophy he had always been a Federalist. Nevertheless, although he believed in an effective national government he was a thoroughgoing democrat. He considered that all the power of the government was derived from the people, and that the real foundation of the government was the character of the people.

His college was very proud of him. The trustees could not praise him too highly, and their determination to keep him at any cost was strengthened by the reputation he was gaining over the country and the offers he was receiving from other institutions. In spite of this atmosphere of warm appreciation he was profoundly discontented with things as they were at Princeton. The changes he wanted seemed to him vital, and although those in the faculty who agreed with him were in the majority and he was admittedly their leader, after all he was only a professor and his power was much limited. Nevertheless, the following years were filled with even more than his usual activity, and he strove incessantly to bring about better conditions in his college. Everything became too intense, and his wife and friends persuaded him, in the summer of 1899, to take another short vacation in Europe.

Again he visited only England and Scotland; and it was very much the same order of trip that had refreshed him before. His brother-in-law, Stockton Axson, went with him, and they had a perfect orgy of delicious relaxing sentiment over Burns' home. His companion was actually reduced to tears as he sat in Burns' chair; and Wilson, with all his humour, would have deeply resented any one's reminding him that Burns was usually under the table instead of in the chair. After leaving the Burns country they rode their bicycles through the Lake region; and Wilson returned to America as well as he had ever been.

He was busy again over the problems of his college and was writing much for popular reading. Many articles were contributed to the magazines dealing with the political life of the nation.

To be effective he laboured to make what he wrote beautiful as well as true; and in the attempt to become an expert artificer in words he relaxed his pursuit of serious scholarship. No one recognized this better than he did, for he was too thorough an historian not to realize that much of what he was writing was the result of a restlessness seeking here and there an outlet.

His writings were not, as he thought, reaching a big public — scholars perhaps, but not politicians; and not the great mass of average humanity. When, among friends, the talk became personal it was apt to turn to his writings. One evening, discussing style, I said, " After forty years your style is yourself — as much so as the shape of your hands. You couldn't, you shouldn't try to change it. In the impersonal outside world the form in which the writers, dear to us, clothe their thoughts is like a familiar face, and you know how the public estimates your writing." He laughed a little wistfully, "You are thinking of a man who has arrived; I, of one imprisoned in a task."

Then the unexpected happened — the tide came his way and he was ready.

V

PRESIDENT OF PRINCETON UNIVERSITY

All things are at odds when God lets a thinker loose on this planet.

Emerson

Chapter Five

PRESIDENT OF PRINCETON UNIVERSITY

THE growing dissatisfaction with things as they were at Princeton was greater among the trustees and the majority of the faculty than Wilson, the leader of the discontents, realized. He felt too much the inertia of old custom and feared that nothing would be done. When, therefore, on June 9, 1902, he was unanimously elected to the presidency, it came with a shock of surprise.

When he wrote to me of his election my feeling was one of dismay. I felt that it would be fatal to his ever writing a great book on government, and that a fine research mind, capable of doing what he alone could do, would be wasted in executive work which many others would do equally well. As was said of a brilliant woman by an irate admirer when she was offered the head-mistresship of a girls' school, "It was like using a razor to sharpen a lead pencil." Impulsively I wrote him to that effect. His answer showed characteristically his estimate of personal and official values.

PRINCETON, 12 July, 1902

"Your letter from Cambridge touched me very near the quick. I have received hundreds of letters about my election to the presidency of the University, and many of them have been from very dear friends, but yours struck a note unlike any of the rest, and roused in me a special sort of gratitude. *You* were thinking of *me*, — of the office hardly at all; the rest of the office chiefly and of their pleasure that I should have been honoured with it. It is not egotism that I should like your way best. You give me a friendship which is for *myself*, — and that I crave more than all the honours and all the praises it were possible to win. — You need give yourself no concern about the History [A History of the American People]. It was finished a couple of weeks ago (no, — one week ago) and my decks are clear; and, as for my health, that is firm and excellent. No doubt I shall have to give up writing for the next three or four years, and that is a heartbreaking thing for a fellow who has not yet written the particular thing for which he has been training all his life; but when I can tell you the circumstances I am sure that you will say that it was my duty to accept. It was a singularly plain, a *blessedly* plain, case."

It was not the " blessedly plain case " it seemed; but it was, what neither he nor any one else could foresee, the rough road to his political goal. His reasons for accepting the office are clear — he had fretted himself ill over his inability to put his ideas for the college into effect, and now had come the opportunity to make Princeton a great national American university.

When he became President of the University, if he seemed autocratic, it must be remembered that he was elected on a reform ticket. He had held a professorship at Princeton for twelve years, was thoroughly familiar with conditions there, and had given his views with extreme frankness. He was the leader of the progressive members of the faculty; in choosing him as chief executive the trustees placed the stamp of their approval on his group, knowing that they might expect rapid and drastic changes. They believed and he believed that they were in entire accord, and neither recognized until much later a fundamental difference among them as to what they chiefly valued in the quality of the University.

On that June day he felt the thrill of the happy warrior. He was entering a fresh field of opportunity with such intense exhilaration and hope that it was like a renewal of life. At last he could do something more than urge reforms; he could realize them. His style and his oratory ceased to trouble him; they would now be used automatically. No longer would he be just a theorizing professor, not to be taken seriously by practical men. To be sure his circuit was still only academic, but if he could not personally enter the political field he could see that youth was trained into citizenship; his university would be a feeder to the national life. He was happier, gayer than he had ever been in his life, or than he was ever to be again. In his inaugural address he took for his title practically the same one he had used for his sesqui-centennial address years before, "Princeton for the Nation's Service." Princeton never lacked enthusiasm on a gala day. Boys trained on the football field give full voice to their side; and Wilson, who never understood the boy, was exhilarated, intoxicated, by the burst of enthusiasm for him. Surely he could mould these youths to his ideals. He forgot that he did not know the individual average boy; he only knew boys in groups; and they only knew him as an inspiring figure in the lecture room.

The trustees and the faculty were almost as exhilarated as the student body. It was the biggest day, the biggest company, the biggest man ever known in American history. Orange and black flags waved; the Tiger roared "Old Nassau"; every one was on the crest of the wave. It was very gay and very young and, to a few of the foreign delegates, a little queer. " Wilson is quite all right," said one of them, " and his ideas are not bad; but after all he is not God Almighty and Princeton is not a throne. I don't wonder that you Americans get on with such a start as you give each other."

If at the ceremonies there seemed over-exaltation, his oration was far from mere oratory; it could be read in quiet far away from the glamour of his presence, and in every half dozen lines there would be found a balanced thought, a new suggestion, an appraisement of value. The architectural character of his mind is lucidly revealed in all his writings and addresses but never more clearly than in this inaugural address. A central idea is placed on a firm foundation and the structure is built upon it, everywhere keeping in touch with the idea, symmetrical, beautiful, convincing. His thesis is that the University is merely a part of the national life. " This is not the place," he says, " to teach men their specific tasks except their tasks be those of scholarship and investigation; it is the place to teach them the relation that all tasks bear to the work of the world." And, " We are not put into this world to sit still and know; we are put into it to act."

In this address he struck the note he had struck as a boy, and his whole life harmonized with that note until his death. It was that neither art nor science nor literature nor any other thing that entered into the making of a man was of value unless it gave him power, to be used for the benefit of humanity. High purpose, vast thoughts, must come to earth and help build the world's highway. In the great game of life with, to most of us, its bewildering shadows and illusive lights, he was not confused or bewildered by either the one or the other; he saw a certain light and followed it with unhesitating steps.

He placed before his audience the University as he visualized it, beautiful in form, with a graduate college in its centre to be the heart of its intellectual life. He referred to his tutorial plan and to his determination to raise the standard of scholarship and morality and to bring an end to all special privileges. Without tact or evasion he placed his cards face upward on the table, and they meant the reorganization of the University from top to bottom. No one, after this could with any justice accuse him of inconsistency. Curiously, what seemed to many Wilson's greatest weakness, his lack of diplomacy, was to be his greatest asset in advancing his own public life.

Wilson put his ideals before an audience with such force that he carried thinking men and women with him. But he was unconscious of the fact that in a mass of people the figure-head is all they can fix their attention upon; it is the man, not his purpose, that thrills them. The politicians were well aware of this and always endeavoured, unsuccessfully, to use him for their own advantage. He could never consciously have played up to their rôle; it was his cause that absorbed him, not himself.

The fates were queerly at work. In the audience sat Colonel George Harvey, editor of *Harper's Weekly* and *The North American Review*. It is reported that he said, " A man who could make an address like that could move the masses of the common people." From that time he kept his eye on Wilson as a promising candidate for the presidency of the United States. He saw the dramatic effect and felt Wilson's power; he failed to see the man.

Present at the inaugural ceremonies, I noticed with amusement the high swish of the waves of glorification until out of the billows there seemed to emerge a spectacular superman; and he, the man, was so very simple. As he sat on the platform his eye every now and then caught that of some (in the worldly sense) quite insignificant friend, man or woman, and the glance between them was the intimate one they would have shared in the home circle.

Wilson's life as president of the University was less spontaneous than it had been during his professorship. In the earlier period the chief worries had been the evils he saw and could not eliminate. Now power was in his hands and the worry was that of responsibility. It was what he wanted; but with his intensity of purpose, the magnitude of the schemes and his lack of strength, he burnt himself out in the doing.

Added to all the college cares were cares at home. Where his affections were concerned he had an unusual capacity for joy or suffering. A few months after his inauguration his father, who had been spending the last years of his life with him, died. He wrote me:

". . . it has quite taken the heart out of me to lose my life-long friend and companion. I have told you what he was to me. And now he has gone and a great loneliness is in my heart. No generation ahead of me now! I am in the firing line! The more reason to be steady and attend to the fighting without repining."

Their lives had been in complete accord; there were never any differences between them and there was great love. As a young man, with the pressing interests of a young man, he found time systematically to help his father write the minutes of the General Assembly of the Church, and he thought the dull work a pleasure. He steadily lightened the road for his father until the journey's end. In these Princeton days the fighting president would, on his return from his official duties, run up to his father's room and sing to him the hymns he loved. He wrote these lines for his father's tomb:

> Steadfast, brilliant, devoted, loving
> and beloved. A master of serious
> eloquence, a thinker of singular
> power and penetration, a thoughtful
> student of life and of God's purpose,
> a lover and servant of his fellow men,
> a man of God.

Had his father survived him he might readily have applied the same words to his son.

The orthodoxy of Woodrow Wilson's faith strengthened him to believe that death could not separate him from his father; and always he kept in his heart the simple village atmosphere of his boyhood. I find in many of his letters such notes as this:

"I am spending the quietest sort of a Sunday here [at Norfolk, Va.].

I have just come from church . . . where I heard a really excellent old-fashioned sermon, — and I feel (except for the hotel) as if I had fallen once again into the slow-paced Southern life which seems to me the most natural of all."

And in another letter of an earlier date:

"I am rested, mind and body, after the morning in church. How seriously quiet Life's waters seemed when there. Over and over again I have thought of those beautiful verses of Keats' you read to me. I am ashamed to say I had never read them; but Ellen, of course, had; and we read them over and we were both back in our childhood homes,

'And moving, with demurest air,
To even-song, and vesper prayer.'"

These are the lines, from the *The Eve of Saint Mark*, he referred to:

Upon a Sabbath-day it fell;
Twice holy was the Sabbath-bell,
That call'd the folk to evening prayer;
The city streets were clean and fair
From wholesome drench of April rains;
And, on the western window panes,
The chilly sunset faintly told
Of unmatur'd green vallies cold,
Of the green thorny bloomless hedge,
Of rivers new with spring-tide sedge,
Of primroses by shelter'd rills,
And daisies on the aguish hills.
Twice holy was the Sabbath-bell;
The silent streets were crowded well
With staid and pious companies,
Warm from their fire-side orat'ries;
And moving, with demurest air,
To even-song and vesper prayer.

I know of no appraisement of Woodrow Wilson that portrays his ultimate inherited quality as well as do these lines of Keats. Unless you realize it you may study his achievements and his failures, you may see the caricature, you may see the myth; but you will never understand the man, who, when his demon for a cause was at rest, the day's active work done, renewed his strength, just as Antaeus renewed his, by a touch with the soil from which he had sprung. Keats, in the poem above, gives the exact quality of that soil.

Though university problems were absorbing him, at the

bottom of his mind there always lived a man intent on, and critical of, the political affairs of his country. In an address before the Virginia Society in 1904, to an audience almost hysterical in their applause, he denounced the Democratic Party as leaderless, and spoke of Bryan's unfitness intellectually to exercise the great power he had. Harvey heard and bided his time. He abominated Bryan's economic policies; but he did not realize that there were a few striking similarities between Wilson and Bryan. Neither could be bought, and from their convictions of right nothing could move them. If a politician wished to use either he would have to comply with his standards and make as much of it as he could. Opposite poles in quality and intellectuality, these two; but how they could hold an audience! — one with brains controlling his eloquence, the other with Heaven knows what, certainly not brains, controlling his. Both were, on the surface, tempting bait for the bosses.

At this time there was a severe return of Wilson's old neuritis. His right hand was again affected; but, in spite of this, he went to Cleveland to make an address before the Western Association of Princeton Clubs. This was in May, 1906. Soon after his return he suddenly lost the sight of his left eye. A specialist was consulted and the diagnosis arrived at was very distressing; it was decided that he had arterio-sclerosis and that his working days were probably over. A little later a very different opinion was reached; the arterial trouble was now thought moderate and its course not likely to be unduly progressive in the near future. Three months, the specialist believed, would put him in fair working form again — only a warning had been given that he must not overwork.

Wilson always met trouble or sorrow or anything over which he had no control with submission. It was only when the fight was in his hands that he rebelled against defeat. The old heroic poems were almost boyishly congenial to him when he was out for slaughtering an evil or establishing a principle. He was very submissive over the first diagnosis and delightfully reassured when it was softened. Three convalescent months in Europe with his wife and daughter did seem to make him fit again; his eye partially recovered, but it continued all his life a disturbing element. In the autumn he was back, to work in a phenomenal way; the danger signal was ignored.

Mrs. Wilson, who watched him trying to read, saw the difficulty he was having with his eye, and he, noticing her anxiety and distress, laughed reassuringly, saying, "I shall train this eye to behave. Never fear." He had a big handle made for his pen in order to save his hand. At every turn he must have been hampered by physical handicaps; but, as he had taught himself to use his left hand when his right was crippled, he now brought into play every faculty to make his work possible, overcoming his difficulties with such nonchalance and such success that even those nearest to him could not realize the strain he was under; they heard from him only his burning desires for the University.

When Wilson first assumed office the endowment of the University was about $4,000,000, which was far too little for the schemes he had in view. He startled the trustees and the alumni by asking that this be increased to $12,000,000. The amount could not, of course, be raised immediately, but in a comparatively short time enough was guaranteed to enable him to proceed with his preceptorial plan. However, before putting that into effect the entire curriculum underwent a change. The requirements for entrance were made more difficult, and a number of undergraduates were dropped because they had failed in their tests. His popularity with the dilettante boys died; and he became anathema with some parents who felt that money could open any door. Without a touch of radicalism he was rather unfair to boys who came up to Princeton from fashionable boarding schools. He told the story of a young freshman who came to his office very rosy and smug, and smartly dressed. "I asked him," he said, "not very seriously, but by way of putting him at his ease, 'What do they teach you boys at your school?' 'They teach us to be gentlemen,' was his pompous reply. I could have kicked the young idiot; but I only said, 'You must add a little Latin and mathematics to your course.'" It was not the individual boy that he was concerned about but the type. The young gentleman of the above incident might have been the son of the most influential man in America, and Wilson would have forgotten him and his name as he left the room. He rarely dwelt on the faults of an individual or condemned a particular school; but he condemned the type of institution that produced an objectionable type of boy. Special privilege he could not endure and he sensed it everywhere in the air about him. His mind was centred on the great masses of people between the two classes, the idle rich and the idle poor. In any class the drunkard, the thief, the ne'er-do-well, found him entirely cold; he could never overcome the feeling that no man need be that way. He would not have gone out seeking the lost sheep, but he would have protected with his life the sheepfold against the wolves. This attitude refers only to his official actions, for, with regard to his personal friends, he was far too much concerned; nor was he callous to any individual if he crossed his path and asked his help.

Among the many anecdotes told of Wilson one is certainly distorted; and as it has been repeated by several of his biographers it seems worth setting straight. A woman had gone to him in great agony over her son's pending dismissal from college. She begged that he might be permitted to remain, saying that she was on the point of submitting to a major operation and she certainly would not live through it with the burden upon her heart of her son's disgrace. Wilson is reported to have said, "Your death, my death, your son's death, count for nothing in comparison with the life of the University. He must go." He could not conceivably have said that in that way. And when I, having heard the tale, laughingly said to him, "The presidency seems to have developed you into a bit of a tyrant," he answered, "You know the sentimental ass I am. Of course I said nothing of the kind. I was wretched and apologetic before that poor woman. The boy had to go but I made it as easy for his mother, and for him, as the circumstances allowed. There are hideous duties that come to you in the course of your life; but no duty need make a man a stupid brute. You know, too, that I fundamentally disbelieve in ruthlessness." Mrs. Wilson told me that he came home ill after that interview, but the woman went home, I am sure, heartened. It would have been impossible for him to treat with rudeness a woman, or any one else, who came to him in trouble. He was, at times, aloof or indifferent, but never inconsiderate. After all, we do not go about in masks; ultimately the world knows what we are; and what is related as our words or deeds, unless they bear our own unmistakable hall-mark, may be put down as counterfeit.

No university president ever had a stronger backing from his trustees than Wilson; and the majority of the faculty were his friends. When he worked out his plan for reorganizing the curriculum they staunchly supported him.

Wilson's idea of what education should accomplish is best given in his own words, extracted from an article on *University Training and Citizenship* in *The Forum* of 1894:

> In order to be rational, a university should have . . . instruction in the history and leading conceptions of those institutions which have served the nation's energies in the preservation of order and the maintenance of just standards of civil virtue and public purpose. These should constitute the common training of all its students, as the only means of schooling their spirits for their common life as citizens. . . .
>
> It is the object of learning, not only to satisfy curiosity and perfect the spirits of individual men, but also to advance civilization. . . .
>
> Every man sent out from a university should be a man of his nation as well as a man of his time. . . .

Whatever he desired to bring about had national bearing. He might be considered America's pioneer in recommending for every boy's first educational consideration, the State.

The financial programme of the University under way and the curriculum in shape, he began putting the preceptorial system into effect. It had been at the back of his mind from the time he began academic work; and after his visits to Oxford and Cambridge in 1896 and 1897 the system had developed into full structural form. Though it caused a vast amount of discussion, pro and con, it was put into operation within an incredibly short time.

A saying regarding the four leading Eastern colleges had been going the rounds. It compared Harvard, on account of its elective system, to a dinner *à la carte;* Yale to a *table d'hote;* Columbia, to a quick lunch; and Princeton, to a picnic. There was so much truth in this ridicule that Wilson's known determination to make Princeton an intellectual centre seemed naïve optimism. He had parodied the old proverb into: "You can send your boy to college but you can't make him think." Nevertheless that was exactly what he intended to do. He told the alumni, at a dinner in New York, "I am not going to propose that we compel the undergraduates to work all the time, but I am going to propose that we make the undergraduates want to work all the time." He believed it of the first importance that the students be interested in their work and that the preceptorial system would be a step to bring that about. He would break up the system of class exercises, so deadening to initiative and scholarship, and have small groups of students meet with preceptors who would discuss with them the subject of their work and advise and encourage them in their reading. Merely cramming a textbook was of little value. The preceptors were to be young men of promise who were looking forward to an academic career. As early as August, 1905, he had engaged forty-seven young men, all of whose records for scholarship and character he had carefully considered, and in the autumn of that year the plan was launched. Its success was instant. A few new and able professors had to be found and in this he was more fortunate than he deserved to be. Often he acted on a quick liking for a man, endowed him with qualities he felt convinced he had, and engaged him — occasionally to the surprise of the candidate.

He then turned his attention to the architectural problems. New laboratories, dormitories, and in time, a graduate college, must be built. Again we see the influence of

Oxford and Cambridge; the buildings must be beautiful and bear some relation to each other. It was largely due to him that Ralph Adams Cram was appointed supervising architect, and some unity of architecture was imposed upon the new buildings.

But his love of the beautiful in architecture was subordinate to his desire to have all the advantages of the college available to the man of small means. As for the sons of rich men, if they came to Princeton, it would be entirely to their advantage to live in simple surroundings; and perhaps the influence of the college might be such as to send them out into the world for a life of service instead of one of ease. His idealism at first flooded the University; but when it reached the point of drastically interfering with the upper class clubs, then the tide changed. He entirely underestimated, he hardly understood, the temptations of weakness and self indulgence and the arrogance that comes from always having had a box ticket. From the time his real attitude towards life was felt the lines of battle were drawn — democracy of opportunity on one side and the rights of privilege on the other.

The evil influence of the social clubs at Princeton was becoming more and more evident. They had developed naturally from earlier conditions, and had become of first importance in the life of the undergraduates. What was to be done about them?

The early American colleges, modeled after the English college, answered well as long as the number of students remained small; but when the student body increased it was inevitable that it should break up into groups, and that class organizations and secret societies should develop. When McCosh abolished the secret societies at Princeton the students formed eating clubs where they could dine together among friends of their own choosing. Gradually these clubs grew into exclusive social organizations, restricted to the two upper classes. They built luxurious club houses on Prospect Avenue, dominated the social life of the college and gave Princeton the reputation of being "the pleasantest country club in America." Democracy seemed to the golden youths to be only a step down in life.

During the first two years of college the students were largely absorbed in scheming for election to a club and were on tenter hooks of anxiety; for only about two-thirds of their number "made" one. Election was entirely independent of scholarship; it was based on social relations, and the clubs furnished a disproportionately small number of honour men. "The evident peculiarity of this life is that it severs the social from the intellectual interests of the place," wrote Wilson. He had steadily insisted that the purpose of the University was intellectual, whereas the social life of the place dominated the minds of the students.

During his summer abroad in 1906 his mind dwelt persistently on matters which seemed to him of first importance for his next constructive move: the remedy for the bad influence of the clubs and the proposed graduate college. He was convinced that the trustees and members of the faculty had, with few exceptions, sympathetically and generously given him a free hand and accepted his leadership; so it was without fear of failure that he pushed the plans that had long been in his mind. He had seen, at the English colleges, students on familiar terms with professors, and freshmen and seniors living together in harmony; and here, in democratic America, in his very own domain, were those abominable, exclusive clubs, and the freshman isolated with his own grade of ignorance. Cambridge and Oxford had put dreams into his head which were to become nightmares, and were to be his undoing — and his making.

At the meeting of the Board of Trustees on December 13, 1906, Wilson reported the good fortune that had followed them in the past four years. Large sums had been donated to the University; the preceptorial system, after a year's trial, was a success beyond their highest expectations and had come to stay; there was a distinct rise in the intellectual level of the undergraduates. What had been done had been well done; but what still remained to be done they knew, and he knew, was of vital importance. Mrs. Thomson Swann's bequest of $250,000 would soon be available for building the proposed graduate college, which would be placed in the midst of the University campus, in the heart of the undergraduate world. But, more to be worked out than anything else, was a remedy for the evil they knew was in their midst, the increasing luxury and undemocratic spirit of the upper class clubs which were affecting disastrously the entire academic body. When Wilson was traveling through the West he had found the Western alumni deeply dissatisfied with the clubs and urging reforms; the non-club men were being made to feel that Princeton was not their college. Important social functions at Commencement and other reunions were conducted by the clubs and many of the Western alumni felt themselves left out in the cold; they felt that money and not brains was in control. It was a wretched state of affairs. All this he placed before the Board with much force and detail. The remedy he was going to ask them to consider would take years to materialize, but he wanted to work definitely towards that end. Summing up his ideas he said:

"The remedy I suggest is, to make the undergraduates live together, not in clubs but in colleges. I propose that we divide the University into colleges and that the strong upper class clubs themselves become colleges under the guidance of the University. By a college I mean not merely a group of dormitories, but an eating hall as well with all its necessary appointments where all the residents of the college shall take their meals together. I would have over each college a master and two or three resident preceptors, and I would have these resident members of the faculty take their meals with the undergraduates. But I would suggest that the undergraduates of each college be given a large share of the self-government in the spirit of our later development, so that the rules of college life should be administered, if not formulated, by committees upon which the undergraduates should have full representation. Each college would thus form a unit in itself, and largely a self-governing unit."

Though the trustees had known Wilson's ideas in general and had regarded them as belonging to the far future, the gravity of the situation came home to them afresh. The evil lay close to a vital part of the University and the remedy proposed was a major operation. The trustees appointed a committee of their number, with Wilson as chairman, to consider the subject and to report back to them.

Wilson's success at Princeton so far had been unprecedented. He was greatly loved by many and recognized by all as a man of power. He had back of him an appreciative Board of Trustees and a loyal faculty; there was no reason in evidence why he should not continue his constructive work rapidly and successfully. The sky seemed to be clear and to indicate clear weather ahead.

After the meeting of the Board, exhausted by overwork, he went for a month's rest to Bermuda, where he quickly recovered his health. And, free from responsibility, he was able to prepare a course of lectures to be given at Columbia

University, which later formed the basis of his important book, *Constitutional Government in the United States.* In it are to be found his most mature thoughts on the subject.

During his absence, the quad system, so-called because the proposed colleges were to be built in quadrangular form around a central court, had absorbed the thoughts of students, faculty, alumni and trustees; and opposition had developed.

Many of the students were beginning to recognize the bad influence of the clubs, and a group, themselves members of clubs, soon after Wilson's return from Bermuda, asked the President and a few members of the faculty for advice. Wilson caught fire at once and called Professor Garfield, Dean Fine and Dr. Paul van Dyke into consultation. When they met in his office he took a small roll of blue paper from his pocket, spread it out and showed them a drawing of the quad plans. He said, " I had not expected to bring this about for twenty-five years, but now the way is opened to us; we shall have the support, not the opposition of the clubs." Garfield and Fine sympathized with Wilson's ideas, but van Dyke had been one of the founders of the Ivy Club, was much attached to it and was not in the least impressed with Wilson's quads. He felt they would destroy the individuality of the clubs — and, in short, it could not be done.

The Committee of the Trustees presented a long report to the Board at its meetings on June 10, 1907. The report reviewed the effect of the clubs on the undergraduates and showed that the tendencies were such that " The vital life of the place will be outside the University and in large part independent of it." The Committee recommended " the grouping of the undergraduates in residential quadrangles," and added further, " It is a choice between one sort of social transformation and another, and this is clearly the time when the choice must be made." Wilson's plans were completely supported by the Committee. The trustees accepted the report with a single dissenting vote, and Wilson felt himself authorized to proceed to develop his plans. But before he went away for his summer vacation in the Adirondacks there had been enough skirmishing in the ranks for him to realize the situation was grave. During the summer the fight waxed hot and acrimonious. Heartening letters came to him, however, from members of the Board and from others; he knew that his trustees were as much actuated by principles as he himself was, and that his ideas of a democratic university were theirs. Consequently he was not deterred by the ominous attitude of the opposition, even though two men as important as Dr. Henry van Dyke and Professor Hibben visited him during the summer and tried to convince him of the hostile mood of the club men and of many of the Eastern alumni. Hibben only wanted him to bide his time; van Dyke was entirely out of sympathy with the quad plan. They could come to no agreement. It was a strenuous summer. Bombarded by friend and foe, Wilson was hardly fit to undergo the ordeals awaiting him on his return to the University.

In the autumn three important faculty meetings were held to discuss the quad plan. We have an account of them in the unpublished diary of Dr. William Starr Myers, then a preceptor, now Professor of Politics, at Princeton:

Thursday, September 26, 1907.

The question of the "Social Coördination of the University"—President Wilson's plan to abolish or transform the upper class clubs, was precipitated in faculty meeting this afternoon. Wilson broached it at commencement time, and it has been agitating faculty, students and alumni since. This afternoon Daniels offered a resolution endorsing the plan and providing for the appointment of a faculty committee to aid the President in carrying it out. Seconded by " Granny " Hunt. Henry van Dyke offered another resolution to throw the whole thing to a joint committee of faculty and trustees for investigation, which every one looks upon as a veiled hit at " Woodrow ". Seconded by " Jack " Hibben and McLenahan. The air was electric for a few minutes, but the whole thing has been put over till an adjourned meeting next Monday afternoon. There will be fun then.

Monday, September 29.

At faculty meeting. Fine debate of two hours. The opposition voted down 81 to 23. Fine speeches by them — Paul van Dyke calling upon Wilson in a frank sincere speech, — and asking him to deal openly with them, and also with the alumni. This called forth from the President one of the most wonderful speeches I have ever heard. I shall never forget him standing there erect behind the desk, the gavel (mallet head) grasped in his right hand, with the end of the handle occasionally placed firm against the top of the desk as he leaned slightly forward in the earnestness of his plea, and his voice occasionally thrilling with an unusual amount of *visible* emotion (for him) — while he stated his dignified position that the faculty must express its opinion without publicly " investigating ", before he could go before the students and alumni in advocacy and explanation of his idea. The whole thing in superb language and diction. A truly wonderful man.

Monday, October 7.

Another faculty meeting, mainly taken up by a superb speech of 1½ hours by President Wilson in explanation of his " quad " plan, or " Idea " as he prefers to call it. He stated that of the *Club* men, 9.63% were honour men,—of the non-Club men, 41.7% were honour men!

In a letter accompanying these notes Dr. Myers writes: "This speech (Sept. 29) not only was the greatest I ever heard Wilson make, but one of the greatest I *ever* heard, if not the greatest. The faculty *cheered* him at the close and I *saw* Dean West heartily applauding it."

The trustees met on October 17 and decided to reconsider their action taken in June. They asked the President to withdraw his recommendations for the quads, and discharged the Committee having this matter in hand. The vote again was practically unanimous, only one vote being cast in favour of Wilson.

What was the cause of this complete about-face of the trustees? We can readily see certain conditions that must have influenced them. They were men of large affairs and the country was then in a state of severe business depression; it would have been very difficult to raise the large sums necessary to erect the college buildings. The University was running an annual deficit which had to be made up by gifts, mainly from the trustees and alumni. All this was known to the Board when, earlier, they had almost unanimously endorsed Wilson's plans; but what they had not anticipated was that the wealthy alumni of the East would be violently in opposition, even to the extent of withdrawing their financial assistance, and that the discussions would divide alumni and faculty into strongly antagonistic groups. In fact they had not reckoned on the storm they were bringing on themselves.

Though the majority of the faculty and a large body of the undergraduates supported the President, the opposition of the Eastern alumni proved the more effective. This confirmed Wilson's assertion that the clubs had become more important than the University, or, as he had earlier expressed it, "The side show had swallowed up the circus."

In spite of their action the trustees did not lose their regard for and appreciation of Wilson; at the instance of Cleveland Dodge they left him entirely free to try and convince the alumni and all he could of the wisdom of his plans. Heartened by the sympathy and strong support of many friends, he determined to go on with the fight, carrying it to the outside world, to the alumni throughout the land; and to return with sufficient backing to convince the Board. Nevertheless the issue was dead and the clubs still flourish at Princeton.

Dr. Harry A. Garfield said to me regarding the Princeton fracas, "I think he is right in what he wants but I think he is wrong in the way he is going about to obtain it. But the brilliancy of his thought and the honesty of his purpose put him ahead of his time; and something greater will be accomplished by him than more opportune fellows ever will accomplish." Only now are the Eastern colleges feeling the influence of Wilson's ideas.

In the country at large Wilson was beginning to lead in an age that was becoming more and more democratic. This is clearly shown by the fact that it was his defeat in the fight for democracy and against privilege at Princeton that brought him prominently before the country and led to the presidency of the United States.

What cruelly hurt Wilson in the Princeton controversy was the opposition of Hibben, for years his closest friend. They had discussed together every question concerning the University, and had seemed to be in complete agreement. Then, at the critical moment in the quad fight,

Hibben cast his vote with the opposition. Wilson felt his bosom friend had betrayed him and he was stunned. " The President's look of shocked amazement was," said an on-looker, " rather terrible." Much of the mystery of the situation is shown by Wilson's surprise and shock, as theirs had been a confidential association for years. Bewildered and not understanding, he was thrown back on himself. Mrs. Wilson wrote me that the break in this friendship was one of the greatest tragedies of his life; and his daughter, Margaret, in a recent letter, writes, " The two major tragedies in Father's life were his failure to carry over the League of Nations and the break with Mr. Hibben." This being the case the episode assumes importance. One thing is certain, that it was no trivial or petty reason, such as a difference of opinion, that caused Wilson to act entirely out of character and, for the first and only time in his life, allow anything to come between him and a close friend. Unquestionably he convinced himself that it was a failure in friendship on Hibben's part. To me the misunderstanding seems to have arisen from the dissimilarity in the natures of the two men: Hibben, given to compromise, tactful and diplomatic; Wilson, the most ardent of advocates could not endow with tact or diplomacy; Hibben with a warm and friendly nature; Wilson, with an intensity of nature that cared for everybody and everything too much. He failed to understand the psychology of his friend, who was neither a Judas nor a Jonathan, nor, one would imagine, a man who would give his life for what he thought was a losing cause. He believed Wilson's ideas right in theory but when the storm of opposition arose he thought them impracticable and not, at that time, conducive to the well-being of the University. Wilson suffered the loss of his friend through his own limitations; he created a figment in his mind and then was bitterly disappointed when instead of his imaginary creation the real man rose and spoke.

Both men had strong partisans and devoted families who took up their advocacy much too zealously. It might well be that, if left entirely to themselves, they would have reached an understanding.

It is an immense pity that this personal sorrow should have come to Wilson at the time that it did. It accentuated the cleavage between his academic and his political life; the disappointments of the former were rendered more acute and the honours that came to him in the latter lost some of their zest.

It puzzled Wilson that Grover Cleveland should have joined the side of the exclusive set; he could not understand that at all. Cleveland had served two terms as President of the United States. He had improved the Civil Service; he had held the country to the gold standard; he had committed his party to a lower tariff. By his rugged integrity and strength of character he had won the respect of the country. Wilson had written of him in 1907, ". . . the men who assess his fame in the future will be no partisans, but men who love candour, courage, honesty, strength, unshaken capacity, and high purpose such as his." After his retirement from office the former President had taken up his residence in a beautiful home in Princeton and had been elected a trustee of the University. But what had become of his democracy? His companions at Princeton were far from belonging to the masses. The old Democrat had done a fine work for the country; now in his retired age he wanted most of all to be let alone, to go fishing or hunting, and enjoy some luxury and easy-going, pleasant companionship. There is no doubt that Wilson's burning zeal for reforms — unpractical reforms, he thought — bored him. " Why? " Wilson wondered and was puzzled.

While Wilson was carrying his fight for the quad system to the alumni throughout the country another serious problem had to be met. The Graduate College had been Dean West's project originally and he had worked unceasingly to secure the necessary money with which to build and endow it. During the lethargy of the Patton régime the trustees had given him almost independent powers to develop his ideas. At the beginning of Wilson's presidency he and West had been in entire accord: undergraduate matters should receive first attention, and the Graduate College, when built, should be located on the campus. Now many reforms had been made and West felt the time was ripe for his College. And here was Wilson pushing the quads and relegating the College to the future.

Wilson and West had both been to Oxford and had talked together of Oxford's entrancing beauty and wondered how they might eventually bring some of that beauty to Princeton. Neither quite realized that two very different spirits were at work.

One cannot help smiling, deadly serious as it was at the time, at the contrast of the plans sponsored by the two. West wanted to place glorified scholars in a palace of ease, well separated from the undergraduates, their rooms heated with wood fires and a private bathroom for each. During his two years at the Johns Hopkins Wilson had noted the intellectual stimulus the advanced students exercised upon the undergraduates, and he wanted a graduate college in the heart of the University in close contact with the undergraduates. He wanted it simple and available to serious students, even though they were men of very moderate means. West and Wilson were in no sense close friends, and as time went on the difference in their ideals steadily increased until it led to open warfare between them.

The West faction was vigorously pushing the Graduate College, for which a donation of $500,000 had been offered provided it were put on a site away from the campus and satisfactory to the donor. Dean West would have the deciding voice in its destiny. The plans were extravagantly beautiful and luxurious. It was apparently to be a graduate club outdoing all the other clubs. This arrangement would entirely destroy the unity of the University and take from the proper authorities the control of its future development. Wilson again put up a desperate fight; the College must stand in the middle of the University, not apart. He actually succeeded in convincing the Board that the $500,000 should be refused unless the trustees should have complete control over its use. Princeton was aghast! To throw away $500,000 for a democratic principle was not done by colleges or churches any more than it was done in business. For a little while Wilson won out to the amazement of the country; then $2,000,000 was bequeathed by will to the Graduate College with West one of the executors of the will. Wilson knew he was beaten. It was reasonable for the Board to feel that with all that money the College could be made a benefit even if it were set apart from the undergraduate world. Wilson accepted this defeat as calmly as he could, but he knew that his work for a democratic university was at an end.

Throughout all this bitter struggle Wilson never attacked the person, only the principle. He was utterly free from malice or gossip. To a friend, less dispassionate, who would have reveled in a fight, and who spoke hotly of Cleveland's attitude, his reply was, " I don't understand; we ought to have agreed. We have never had a greater Democratic

President than Cleveland — oh, he is a great man." And then ending, as he usually did, with a humorous smile, "It's sad to admire a man so much and to find he doesn't admire you at all." "Well, what have you to say of West?" his friend continued. "West," he answered. "Now you are more on my level. I should say that West was a little difficult." Then, whimsically, "I suspect he thinks I am too." If one had stood up for West's ideals then indeed there would have been a fusillade, his ideals storming West's. Nevertheless he was very thin-skinned; he took all things too seriously.

He still had many friends in Princeton. So far as the heart is concerned few men have been so faithfully loved, and he had enough hate from his opponents to keep him from becoming soft. But, a very weary man, he apparently put down his arms.

Looking back to that serious shindy of long ago one gets the impression of a frontier fight. The two outstanding leaders, Wilson and West, were both stout fellows, fighters to the death. They both loved Princeton; but Wilson was always nationally minded — "Princeton in the Nation's Service." West thought that a fine phrase, but Princeton came first; no doubt she would serve the nation, but he was concerned with the part of the nation that was called the upper classes — properly so-called, he thought. He firmly believed in special privileges — the more you could honestly get, the better man it marked you out. Each of the two men was working for what he thought was right; and each felt that he was the inevitable leader. Neither would dream of compromising an inch; was he not fighting for the life of the University? Wilson's view was by far the bigger one; it was democratic and epoch-making. As Dr. Garfield wrote to me: "It is plain from the beginning until the end Mr. Wilson's attitude towards life was quickened and determined by the democratic principles so hateful to the old order at Princeton, to the bosses and politicians in state and nation. One could not very well miss his devotion to this underlying principle."

A democratic university was his ideal, and he looked out with clear eyes to the broad problems of the United States. He felt that knowledge led to wisdom and wisdom to righteousness; and that it was a road which all who would, should be able to take without handicap. And so, with a carelessness of self that was amazing, he fought unceasingly that there should be no sign, " Private Property," marked over the great highway.

What renders this ado of more than local consequence is that unconsciously Wilson, merely a university president attempting reforms for his institution, had caught the ear and eye of the country. It was impossible for him to be locally minded; wherever he went his thought overflowed his environment and spread over a field that had no limited boundary lines. It was democracy on trial.

Many whispers came, like the suggestion of his running for the senatorship from New Jersey; but he hardly heard the suggestion; that was not for him. Then it was proposed that he be the candidate for the vice-presidency with Bryan as candidate for the presidency; that seemed to him an utter absurdity.

The question has often been asked: When did Wilson first have the presidency of the United States in view? I am certain it never entered his mind before his governorship of New Jersey. The possibility of it had been mooted in the latter days of his presidency of Princeton, but he did not take it seriously. His desire to lead a political life dated from his boyhood; but the position he would hold if his desire were realized was not defined in his mind. Once, during the Princeton turmoil, Dr. Henry van Dyke said to me, "I do hope that Wilson's foolish friends will not put it into his head that he might become President of the United States." When I told Mr. Wilson of this remark he laughed gleefully and said, "I shall never worry Henry in that way. My! In what a temper it would put him! He would be certain I would attempt to destroy the blessed Constitution." Then he added, rather sadly, "It would be a queer time for me to think of the presidency of the United States when I may not be able to keep the presidency of my University. No, if I think my job at Princeton no longer a useful one I shall get to work on my *magnum opus*." Neither he nor Dr. van Dyke had the gift of true prophesy. Later, when Dr. van Dyke was Minister to Holland, he said, "The country has never been in greater and safer hands than those of Woodrow Wilson."

We who are following the records of Wilson's life see how, during the Princeton presidency, he steadily but unconsciously approached the political field; we see how Colonel Harvey kept his eye upon him; but, more than that, we see why he did. The sweeping and convincing effect of his writings and addresses upon cultivated men like Charles Francis Adams, President Eliot, Walter Hines Page and others of their type, made him an intellectual leader. He spoke to them with the authority of the scholar. Harvey did not undervalue this, but what won him was that, when under great emotion, possessed with a demon for a cause, Wilson rose to the oratory of the evangelical preacher, spoke directly to the people, for the people, in language they understood — his ministerial forebears rioting within him. After his strong rush of addresses through

am so sure you can divine. I dread the possibility and yet feel that I must offer myself and not shirk. Your judgment of Roosevelt is mine own. God save us of another four years of him now, in his present insane distemper of egotism!

Ellen and the girls join me in messages of deep affection. It delighted us so to hear from you. I hope that you have got both health and pleasure amidst your old haunts and friends.

Your devoted friend,

Woodrow Wilson

Alas! The Governor of N.J. (till 1914) cannot

A letter written by Woodrow Wilson to the author and dated Princeton, 26 May, 1912 the colour comes back into the world when a dear friend speaks and calls one's heart back from its anxious quest amongst strangers. Your letter did me a world of good. You are always there, to think about and depend on; but when you speak the comfort and reassurance come in a flood!

The political field is hopelessly confused: no one can confidently predict anything, — not even the nomination of Roosevelt, though that seems daily more probable. On the Democratic side is now looks as if the choice of the convention might lie between Bryan

his bailiwick to travel across seas!

the country, denouncing special privilege, voicing democracy, Harvey was sure of his man.

A strong current was running against the Republican Party which for many years had controlled the Government. Consequently the Democratic bosses of New Jersey were hopeful, if they could find the right candidate, of winning the governorship of the State. Harvey was looking still further ahead; two years as governor would prepare Wilson for the presidency of the United States, and there was no other Democrat who, he thought, had so good a chance of success. But it needed very convincing persuasion to make the bosses believe that Wilson was a winning card. It is curious that Wilson, in spite of his lifelong desire for active political life, hung back. He found it hard to realize that Harvey was truly serious.

When the day of the nomination convention for the governorship was set Harvey brought more and more pressure to bear upon Wilson, and at last convinced him that he was in earnest. Then, as the times seemed very dark at Princeton, Wilson yielded and agreed to accept the nomination with the proviso that he was bound by no promises or obligations. As he said, in his speech of acceptance at the convention: " As you know, I did not seek this nomination. It has come to me absolutely unsolicited, with the consequence that I shall enter upon the duties of the office, if elected, with absolutely no pledges of any kind to prevent me from serving the people of the State with singleness of purpose. Not only have no pledges of any kind been given, but none have been desired."

The political bosses, who had forced through his nomination, thought that fine campaign talk. They were not looking for a good governor but for a good candidate.

Their candidate was an amateur in politics; and they thought they could control him.

At the successive advances in his life Wilson had felt a certain exhilaration, but this time, no. He smiled a little wistfully as he said to me, " Am I equal to this big work when I failed in a much smaller one? " And then, " Yes; I believe I am, for now I shall be speaking to the American people, not to an academic group rooted in tradition and fearful of progress." But the last years had aged him. He had met defeat, or what he felt was defeat; he had encountered serious opposition for the first time; he had seen hostile faces where once there had been only friendly faces: it was his preparation for American political life. " Does he never think himself wrong? " many as of old continued to ask. " Not in the direction I am taking," would have been his answer. There he was sure of himself. " Where the individual should be indomitable is in the choice of direction," he had once said.

VI
GOVERNOR OF NEW JERSEY

The only true foundation for national prosperity is a religious regard for the rights of others.

Isocrates

Chapter Six

GOVERNOR OF NEW JERSEY

RAY STANNARD BAKER gives a spirited and detailed account of the campaign for the governorship. To politicians it may be enlightening; to laymen of mature years who have heard at intervals of four years a deluge of slanders and glorifications — the people the same goat before the altar — mud and flowers intermingled — it gives an appalling sense of an unchanging world. But the aftermath of this particular campaign was unique. Wilson meant what he said and, when elected, actually kept his promises, to the utter disgust of his political supporters.

In his social life when President of Princeton, he felt the nagging influence of village surroundings; all knew one another's affairs, or thought they did, and the women did a lot of damage championing the points of view of their husbands or of their friends. Unfortunately, Wilson allowed the gossip to harass him. The essential issues of his life were driven with even more than his usual impetus because of the nervous fret of it all. During the early years of his presidency there had been too much personal sentiment in his life, his friends too close, his work too quickly successful. Then the reverse and apparent failure. Again his chance had come; there was no sentiment now. The machine politicians were hard-boiled, clever, and in the main self-seeking men who made no demands upon his heart, but kept his mind and his wit on the alert. He was in an atmosphere that strengthened his physical robustness; the prospect of putting his governmental policies into practice greatly invigorated him.

His addresses during the campaign rang with sincerity; he would introduce reforms into the State government and would be the leader of the people. " Those who don't want me as leader," he said, " should not vote for me." All this sounded to the machine bosses fine campaign trumpeting; they had heard it before though not so well done, and they smiled in their sleeves. But the people to whom, in his mind, he was always talking, had watched his selfless fight for democracy at Princeton. They had seen him ready to strip himself of friends, position and means to make good his ideals. They knew that he meant what he said, that he had faith in them and in that fair land which he visualized as America — or what he longed for America to be.

But the reformers of both parties looked at him somewhat askance. They knew that he was the candidate of the Democratic bosses, and they feared that if elected, he, like former candidates, might forget his campaign promises and use his office for the benefit of the machine. A series of questions was addressed to him to discover his attitude to the bosses and to the reform measures then under discussion. His reply was so open and frank, and his condemnation of the machine so definite that he rallied the progressive people of the State, Democrats and Republicans alike, to his support. Even some of the machine politicians were won over by his ability and personality. He was elected by a large majority.

One incident greatly increased his influence. James Smith, the leading Democratic boss of the State, wished to be sent to the United States Senate, contrary to the expressed wishes of the voters at the primaries. It was a question of the supremacy of the people or the supremacy of the machine, and Wilson was determined that the people should control. The issue had not been important during the campaign, as Smith had announced that he would not be a candidate for the Senate. But as soon as the election was over and Democratic success assured, Smith, with utter disregard of his former attitude, sought the pledges of the new members of the State legislature to elect him to the Senate. He even tried to get Wilson's support. At that time senators were elected by the State legislature; the popular election of senators came later. Wilson tried his best, but unsuccessfully, to induce Smith to withdraw. Then, after full warning, he followed his method of appealing to the people. In two crowded meetings in Smith's own bailiwick he denounced him as being not a Democrat, but merely the head of a selfish system, regardless of the interests of the people. He was received with enthusiastic applause. Wilson also discussed the matter with members of the legislature, and when the election took place Smith was ignominiously turned down, and his political power broken.

It looked like a miracle that an academic gentleman, a professor, should beat the bosses in their own field. The explanation is simple: he had equipped himself for just this task and undertook it with a high conscience and a perfect understanding of the psychology of machine methods. With Cleveland he believed that " public office is a public trust." The petty politicians, on the other hand, felt that public office was the gift of the bosses, to be won by loyal service to their organization, to be received with gratitude and used for mutual advantage. Wilson knew that the machine depended largely on patronage, and when he refused to throw the patronage of the State into its hands, it stood aghast with powers greatly curtailed. Furiously the bosses shouted " Ingrate! ". He was not in the least abashed; he had not sought the nomination, he had accepted it, and only with the distinct provision that he was under no obligations to any one. His writings, his addresses, his conferences, all had reflected the principles he would follow. But that any one should seek office except for selfish reasons was beyond the imagination of the machine.

Woodrow Wilson was inaugurated Governor of New Jersey on January 17, 1911. In his inaugural address he voiced his conceptions of the duties of public officials. He said:

" We are servants of the people, of the whole people. Their interest should be our constant study. We should pursue it without fear or favour. Our reward will be greater than that to be obtained in any other service; the satisfaction of furthering large ends, large purposes, of being an intimate part of that slow but constant and ever hopeful force of liberty and of enlightenment that is lifting mankind from age to age to new levels of progress and achievement, and of having been something greater than successful men. For we shall have been instruments of humanity, men whose thought was not for themselves, but for the true and lasting comfort and happiness of men everywhere. It is not the foolish ardour of too sanguine or too radical reform that I urge upon you, but merely the tasks that are evident and pressing, the things we have knowledge and guidance enough to do; and to do with confidence and energy."

Wilson began immediately to push forward the reform bills that he thought were of the first importance: the election bill, the public utilities bill, the corrupt practices bill, and the employers' liability bill. They were all passed before the legislature adjourned late in April; an astonishing feat when we realize that the election bill and the corrupt practices bill were definitely aimed at the machine.

The independent governments of the several States of the Union offer interesting opportunities for trying new methods of government without involving the whole country. From his youth Wilson had stressed the importance of leadership and responsible government; and he now attempted to apply these ideas to the State of New Jersey. His victory over the bosses and the confidence of the masses made him the leader of his party and of the State. By close coöperation between the executive and the legislative branches he laid the foundation for a government responsible to the people. He was governor only two years and in that time, as Dodd writes in his book, *Woodrow Wilson and His Work*, " the laws of the community were so re-made that reformers everywhere studied them as models for other states." Unfortunately, the time was too short to embody changes in the State constitution, and New Jersey has not preserved all the reforms of the Wilson administration. We can only speculate on what would have been the influence of Wilson's ideas on the government of the country if they had taken permanent root in New Jersey.

Wilson's method and successful reforms in his own State were making a deep impression on the country at large; it was grand work he was doing. And about this time upon the scene enters Colonel House of Texas. A Democrat widely known in his own State, trusted and liked by high and low, he had been the adviser of successive governors. His sagacity was a byword; he placed men where they belonged with a peculiar nicety, and his prophetic eye was trained from boyhood by watching the game of politics with an all-absorbing interest; he early took a hand in it for the pleasure it gave him. Now, after ten years' experience he found himself looked upon as an expert consultant by the people of his State — and his eye turned to a bigger field.

The presidential election was to take place a year later, in 1912; and this astute player of men upon the political chessboard had been canvassing the country in his mind for a candidate who could lead the Democratic Party to victory. No one had so much influence with the Democrats of the nation as William Jennings Bryan; but Bryan had led his party to defeat three times and was certainly not a winning candidate. Nevertheless no Democrat could succeed without Bryan's support. Still more was necessary: the candidate must be economically sound to satisfy the East and must be able to arouse the enthusiasm of the masses. Could Bryan be induced to back such a man if such a man could be found? The general dissatisfaction of the country made it a good Democratic opportunity.

After considering several men who might be possible, Colonel House came to the conclusion that the Governor of New Jersey was his best hope. But he must have felt very dubious, for the caricature of Wilson as a pig-headed, self-righteous pedagogue and a ruthless reformer, even though the masses trusted him as their friend, did not seem promising for a presidential candidate. Still, Harvey believed in his star and Harvey was not easily hoodwinked. House would meet Wilson and then make up his mind. And so, prefaced by a few preliminary overtures, the meeting took place, and the liking for each other was instantaneous. They had lunch together and talked over the political situation. It is easy to picture them — Colonel House, intent on sizing up the man before him as a possible candidate; Wilson, wholly delighted, feeling that he had met a kindred soul. Each felt at once that he had found a man to whom he could talk easily and frankly on all subjects, and the friendship was begun. House was extremely likable and could put any man at his ease, and no man was more likable than Wilson when at his ease. Both were absorbed in the political life of the day, and each realized in the other a sincere desire to benefit the country if an opportunity came. Colonel House writes in his diary,

"From the first meeting up to today [1916] I have been in as close touch with Woodrow Wilson as with any man I have ever known. The first hour we spent together proved to each of us that there was sound basis for a fast friendship. We found ourselves in such complete sympathy in so many ways that we learnt to know what each was thinking without either having expressed himself. A few weeks after we had met and had exchanged confidences, which men usually do not exchange except after years of friendship, I asked him if he realized that we had known each other for so short a time. He replied, 'My dear friend we have known each other always.' And I think this is true."

It was very natural for Colonel House to feel that Wilson's attitude towards him was unusual, but such a beginning, in almost the same words, was the experience of all Wilson's close friends. His friendships were made on the instant; there was no slow approach, no weighing of qualities. Many notes bear out this statement and all inquiries bring the same answer: "As soon as we met we were friends." The unusual part was that these affinities often endured; certainly it was so with Colonel House.

Before me lies a note Wilson wrote to a young woman after a first meeting in his college days: "I felt at once that we were intimate friends " it begins. It was true, for when his life was nearing its end he wrote to her, " I long to talk with you. The thought of you cheers me as only the thought of a beloved friend can cheer me now." His daughter writes of his meeting with his English friend, Yates, the painter: " They became friends while standing on a little bridge gazing at Wordsworth's mountains. They both happened to be standing there during the sunset, and Mr. Yates introduced himself to Father with these words, ' My name is Yates, Fred. We live hard by here, my wife and daughters and I. We are poor, but thank God, not respectable.' Father came home chuckling with pleasure over such an introduction, and declared afterwards that from that moment he had always known Yates." And such was the beginning and such the sequel, in almost the same words, of all his near friendships, whether they were made in serious or light moments. Nevertheless it was sincere and durable stuff. The personal outgoing that met a friendly approach came from his fundamental longing for affection.

This warm and human side of Wilson's character apparently surprised Colonel House and increased his liking; he recognized that his chosen candidate had something very lovable about him along with sterner qualities. No jealousies of friend or relative can ever take from Colonel House the memory of the friendship that was his—not possibly. From the time of Wilson's campaign for the presidency to the end of his active life he and Colonel House were in constant consultation on governmental matters. The unlikeness in tradition between the two men worked for their mutual benefit in many ways. Agreeing in principle they met life from different angles. Wilson only wanted the little job of putting the world on a safe basis, and in that desire he and Colonel House met with enthusiastic sympathy and optimism. Theirs was an unbroken alliance until Wilson's physical breakdown. When a man is confined to a sick room, guarded by a jealous and solicitous family, a trained nurse and a private physician, friends may be kept away because it is thought best for the patient, but the patient is in no way responsible.

Few men in history have been more self-assured about their ideas and ideals than Wilson; few more certain that their plans for realizing them were right. Neither Colonel House nor any living man could have affected Wilson in such matters. Where governmental principles were concerned none but dead men influenced him — the great statesmen of the past whose ideas had been tested. Many of those who disagreed with Wilson on fundamentals found him an impregnable fortress, and thoroughly detested him. Hadn't they ideas too — and plans? But he was deaf to their voices and carried his ideas over their heads. Self-assurance is a characteristic all great leaders have — and must have. House recognized Wilson's powers of leadership at once and, fortunately for their comradeship, he agreed with his ideas; he knew that Wilson worked from a knowledge of his subject gained by long years of study. Wilson knew the history of institutions; he knew how our form of government had evolved from experiments and failures in the past, and on these subjects the politicians in general were densely ignorant. House realized that Wilson was not thinking of himself; he was thinking of the country; his canvas was national. And so he decided then and there to employ his wide experience in practical politics to make Wilson's ideas effective. "Never before," he wrote to his brother-in-law, "have I found both the man and the opportunity."

Soon after their first meeting House began his plans to help organize the campaign. Wilson was primarily a statesman, not a politician. It was a great advantage for him to have at his side a friend like House, who quietly looked over the ground and laid out the moves, only looking up to attend to the usual volleys of slanders when one might do harm. He must have smiled to see Wilson and Mrs. Wilson taking any of the stuff to heart. That it was difficult for his candidate to think any man a liar (if he were not a machine politician), though the world was full of liars, did not at first seem very intelligent for so learned a man. Well, House would look after the liars if only he could persuade Wilson not to trust them, or not to knock out at sight one who, with all his tricks, might prove valuable for the campaign.

Among the things that distressed Wilson was the break with Harvey. He valued what Harvey had done for him; he liked him and he believed in him. House and other men interested in the campaign had shown Wilson that the West was putting a wrong construction on Harvey's championship in *Harper's Weekly*, believing that this magazine represented the interests of Morgan and the financial plutocrats. A conference was arranged between Harvey and Wilson in which the former frankly asked Wilson if he thought his advocacy in *Harper's Weekly* was being interpreted as the support of the moneyed classes. Wilson answered as frankly that he thought it was, and was surprised and distressed when later told that Harvey was offended. He wrote him a cordial letter explaining that he had a " one track mind," and that his answer had been simply " a matter of fact," and expressing his appreciation of Harvey's support. Harvey later, though not immediately, ceased to advocate Wilson's candidacy. Between the two there was only a political alliance, insisted upon by Harvey, slowly and reluctantly entered into by Wilson, and dropped by Harvey when things did not go his way. There had been no real friendship between them. The rupture was seized upon by Wilson's opponents and exaggerated for campaign purposes. Referring to these reports Wilson said to his friend, Dr. Hiram Woods, "I felt as though I had been walking through mud. I just do not understand Harvey." Harvey's antagonism, however, had now to be reckoned with by Wilson's campaign managers.

House had seen too many plans miscarry ever to feel sure; to him the best way was carefully to anticipate trouble, and above all to keep the party together. Bryan must be brought to Wilson's aid. At the beginning of the campaign House tactfully brought before Bryan and Mrs. Bryan the work the Governor of New Jersey was accomplishing, with the object of enlisting their interest. This he succeeded in doing, and it was one of the chief factors in securing Wilson's nomination. It was an interesting piece of psychological work, and curiously it was honest; all he said of Wilson was true.

The convention for the Democratic nomination opened in Baltimore on June 25, 1912. Wilson and the other candidates had established headquarters in the city. The fight was on. Wilson's chief rival was Clark of Missouri, and as he had Bryan's backing it looked at first as though he would surely win.

Baltimore's big armoury was packed to the limit to witness a life and death struggle between the progressives and the people on one side, and the politicians and the plutocrats on the other. The New York delegation, controlled by Tammany and including some of the big business men of the country, took their seats, very confident of success. They had ninety votes to deliver and the power of money.

After the convention had been organized and before the candidates were named, up rose old Bryan and justified his title of "Peerless Leader." He had already become a power in the convention, but he made a master stroke when, ignoring all precedents, he offered the following resolution:

> ". . . As proof of our fidelity to the people, we hereby declare ourselves opposed to the nomination of any candidate for President who is the representative of or under obligation to J. Pierpont Morgan, Thomas F. Ryan, August Belmont, or any other member of the privilege-hunting and favour-seeking class."

Such a storm broke loose that even the police could not quell it; but Bryan, in his old black suit and white string tie, was superb. He mopped his head composedly, for the heat was intense and his avoirdupois great, and waited until his voice could again be heard. Then he continued: "This is an extraordinary resolution; but extraordinary conditions need extraordinary remedies . . . 'If thy right hand offend thee, cut it off' . . . If it is worth while to cut off the right hand to save the body, it is worth while to cut off Morgan, Ryan and Belmont to save the Democratic Party." A vote of 883 to 202 proclaimed Bryan's victory. Morgan, Ryan and Belmont, sitting aghast in the front row, must have felt that a nickel had beaten a dollar.

The Democratic National Chairman, McCombs, was from all available accounts a wretchedly poor worm. His advice, invariably bad, was fortunately not taken. If things went wrong he wanted to back out; if they went well he nearly upset them; he gave the effect of a frantically nervous chicken trying to cross a crowded highway. Wilson, at Sea Girt, kept informed of the happenings in Baltimore, refused to follow his advice, and, at a critical moment, sent his nerve-racked Chairman instructions that he would not accept the nomination if it depended on Tammany's vote. Things seemed at a deadlock, with Clark leading but not gaining. Then Bryan, whose Nebraska delegates were voting for Clark, learned that Clark was intriguing for the Tammany vote, and again rose magnificently to the occasion. Amid an amazed audience he made another master stroke — he declared he would vote for no one supported by the New York delegation; he released the Nebraska delegates from their instructions and cast his vote for Wilson.

The old Commoner may have oozed piety and uttered epigrammatic platitudes or economic idiocies, but when he rose and cast his vote for Wilson he was a big man and his audience felt it. From this moment Wilson began to gain and finally obtained the necessary two-thirds vote on the forty-sixth ballot. Then there was a mighty noise in the armoury; flags went up over the city; whistles tooted, and the fight was over with Wilson nominated for President and Marshall for Vice-President.

Bryan beamed on all about him; the people had triumphed over the machine. More than a hundred thousand telegrams from all over the country had been showered upon the delegates. It recalls what Wilson, in 1897, had said of the second nomination of Cleveland, that he " was nominated for the presidency by acclamation, not because the politicians wanted him, but because their constituents did."

When the reporters told Wilson, at his cottage at Sea Girt, of the action of the convention and asked for his comments, he replied, "Say that the news was received in a riot of silence." Nevertheless, he and Mrs. Wilson took the result over-seriously for their good; they got very little pleasure out of it, especially Mrs. Wilson. Her attitude was always true to her traditions, those of a devoted daughter of a Presbyterian manse in a Southern town. A higher position in life meant only greater opportunity for service; and the joy of victory must have seemed small compensation for her suffering during the campaign. With her immense pride in her husband every silly scandal that was flung at him went through her heart. The following extract from a letter written to me after the nomination shows a little how she felt:

Governor's Cottage
Sea Girt, New Jersey,
Aug. 10, 1912

". . . Our life now is indescribably full — swarms of people constantly, and a mountain load of letters to be answered. But "it is all in the day's work" and things are going so bravely now that it would seem a sin to complain of anything. As someone expresses it the country is "in an epidemic of delight" over the Wilson nomination. The very letters which make our life so hard for us are rather wonderful. One of the secretaries has made a careful analysis of them from many points of view — and the result is *most* interesting. Of the 10,000 or more received more than half, by count, state they have prayed for the nomination of Woodrow Wilson. So it would seem that if it was a campaign of *praying versus lying* the odds were on our side after all. We had the "stronger battalions" — those legions surrounding the city which Elijah saw when the Lord opened his eyes."

To Be Or Not To Be.

By permission of The Sun, *Baltimore, Md., and Mr. McKee Barclay*

Prayer, religion, in a political campaign of the twentieth century! One does wonder a little about that.

A few letters to me from the Democratic nominee himself give his own reactions. During the campaign he was oversensitive to the lively criticisms and inventive imaginations of his opponents. One feels, on reading the letters, that he was too thin-skinned and suffered unnecessarily when brought into contact with unscrupulous men. The following extract from a letter dated May 27, 1912, illustrates his mood:

> ". . . Everybody over here seems to agree that there has never been a campaign in which there was such a systematic and malevolent attempt to destroy a man's reputation for character and intellectual integrity as has been made by my opponents all over the country, including the representatives of the other candidates for the Democratic nomination, and in such circumstances one *needs* to hear the voice of true and loyal friends to keep him in heart.
>
> Not that I actually lose heart . . . but the world grows sometimes to seem so brutal, so naked of beauty, so devoid of chivalrous sentiment and all sense of fair play, that one's own spirit hardens and is in danger of losing its fineness. I fight on, in the spirit of Kipling's 'If', but that is oftentimes a very arid air. . . .
>
> The political field is hopelessly confused; no one can confidently predict anything, — not even the nomination of Roosevelt, though that seems daily more probable. On the Democratic side it now looks as if the choice of the convention might lie between Bryan and me. I need not tell you how I feel about it, — I am so sure you can divine. I dread the possibility and yet I feel that I must offer myself and not

shirk. Your judgment of Roosevelt is mine own. God save us from another four years of him *now*, in his present insane distemper of egotism! "

Wilson had been watching political campaigns all his life; he knew they were all of a kind, and yet the nasty mud slinging came too close and he lost his perspective. But with the nomination the strain was over and he realized that he had been chosen by the people. He and the people would ultimately crush the machine.

Sometime after his nomination I showed him two delightful caricatures. One of Roosevelt and Taft, confronting each other and dripping with gore, while exclaiming: " Now just look what *you* done! " The other of Bryan, posed as Hamlet, pondering, " To be or not to be." The Democratic candidate shook with laughter. " They are the ones," he said gleefully, " who gave me the nomination. Do you recall how I wrote you: ' God save the country from another four years of Roosevelt in his insane distemper of egotism? ' Yet what a glorious egotist he is! And old Bryan! No, you are not to make fun of him. I like him."

Wilson's humour had returned; he could now laugh at himself for having taken himself and his adversaries too personally. In the end he was always able to laugh at himself. But his cause was another matter; towards it he was profoundly serious and objective.

The strong political leaders in America, like Wilson, who stick to their oars in spite of the queer stuff piloting them through muddy waters, are few. An isolated group, surrounded by every device the political machine can devise, they remain unseduced. Wilson awaited his election heart to heart with the people, his whole mind given to studying their interests. The interests of the country and that of the mass of the people are identical, he said. Any relegating of one class to the disadvantage of another will ultimately destroy the whole. For a generation or two the privileged group may fatten materially; but the country, to save its life, must harmonize the whole. So, in effect, he talked to his non-political friends, enlarging on the ideas he had always held; as, when President of Princeton, he had fought against special privileges; and when Governor of New Jersey, he insisted on a government of the people by the people. To him it seemed that the whole of history had been a struggling advance along the lines he proposed to follow. He even felt that in his day, and perhaps by his hand, the world might be given such laws that it would be safe for democracy. He longed to do something more definite than leave an ideal. Over and over he might have been heard to say, "Without vision the people perish," but he was devoting his mind to making that vision a certain fact, holding it steady by wise laws. And yet of him no truer words could be spoken than those of Pasteur: "Blessed is he who carries within himself a God, an ideal of beauty, and who obeys it; ideal of art; ideal of science; ideal of the fatherland; ideal of the virtues of the gospel; for therein lie the springs of great thoughts and actions; they all reflect light from the Infinite." Wilson's ideal, "the God within him," was peace and unity of purpose, held down to earth by just laws.

In the campaign for the presidency he simply carried on the same note that had marked the campaign for the nomination. He was elected November 5, 1912. As was customary his opponents gave him the right hand of fellowship — with mental reservations — and bided their time.

Immediately after his election the hungry horde of office seekers began to swarm. He delivered an ultimatum that no important appointments would be made until he was prepared to announce them; and then, wrapping about himself what little mantle of reserve he could gather, he fled with his family to Bermuda for rest and time to think. Before leaving he announced that he would call a special session of Congress early in April in order that his campaign promises might be kept.

After four weeks in Bermuda, trying to keep his thoughts on the essential problems of the country, he returned to New Jersey to find the bosses at work trying to defeat the anti-trust laws he was pushing, counting on his absorption in national affairs, jubilantly thinking that he would have so big a field for his ideas that he would let them alone. To their disgust and discomfiture he threw himself at once into the conflict, announcing that he was Governor of New Jersey until he became President of the United States, and intimating that even after that the whip handle would still be in his grasp. His utterances show the irritation of a man who has been interrupted in an important moment of quiet. It seemed to the nation rather a tempest in a teapot, but to him it seemed an attempt to wipe out all the work he had accomplished in New Jersey. He was very wroth; and no doubt he liked a fight in a good cause. Some of the fine edge of a fastidious scholar had been rubbed off during the years of his governorship; he had been cleaning his State of much dirty water, and he had to put his hand in it. Now, not only were the bosses hot on his heels, but the usual mischief-makers were at work. Many members of his party were uneasy: Wall Street's sensitive temperature might take a drastic fall. It was the usual game of the politician; but Wilson took it seriously. He fought the bosses successfully and his anti-trust laws were passed. He spoke his mind about his opponents with no diplomacy and with very stark truth. To many it seemed unnecessarily rough handling, but he won. The progressives had their belief in him confirmed, and the Chicago business men applauded his stand. These vigorous speeches and the New Jersey fight were perhaps not done in his most finished style, but it was the last time that the naturally impatient man could allow his impatience to have full swing. The successes of the years of the presidency were achieved only with infinite patience.

The next thing for him to consider was the personnel of his Cabinet. He wanted the best men he could get irrespective of politics, but the men he most wanted, Charles Eliot, President of Harvard; Dean Fine of Princeton; Walter H. Page, Louis Brandeis, Newton D. Baker, were, for one reason or another, not obtainable. There was nothing to be done but to consider the material that was available. In this Colonel House did masterly service by gathering information from many sources about the men under consideration. In electing Wilson the people showed that they wanted a progressive government; so he determined, in harmony with his own desires, to appoint only progressives to important political posts, men who could be relied upon to work with him along the lines of his known policies. They were not to be chosen because during the campaign they had rendered important party service — with one exception, William Jennings Bryan.

The placing of Bryan had immediately to be considered. " What will be done with Bryan," was on every one's lips, and there was speculation about it in every newspaper. The East was uneasy and prophesied dire results if Bryan was given a leading position. The West vowed that dire results would happen — they'd see to it — if he was not given the best that could be had. He was their Peerless Leader. Roosevelt had called him a blithering ass; but, with the exception of Bryan's ideas of free silver, he had adopted all the Commoner's policies complete — without a word of acknowledgment.

Wilson had met serious disappointment in forming his Cabinet and he was especially anxious to have an ideal man for Secretary of State. He realized, perhaps more clearly than any other person, that Bryan was far from being the right material for a Cabinet position. His economics were, in Wilson's mind, absolutely unsound; he had no knowledge of the diplomatic world; yet he had been the leader of his party for sixteen years, and Wilson was under great obligations to him. To offend him or his constituents would mean a split in the party and a defeat to the policies of the administration. He was clearly the inevitable choice — yet Wilson hesitated; he had not a drop of opportunism in his composition. It is always a nervous situation for a political party if its head cannot be counted upon to act with the wisdom of the serpent when imperative; but the probabilities are that when a crisis is reached the man will act according to his character. Wilson had given his advisers bad moments: they recalled his naïve frankness with Harvey; then the risk he took when, during the nomination convention, he threw away the New York vote; and they remembered that at Princeton he had thrown over everything for what he thought right. Now how would he treat Bryan?

When men like Wilson and Bryan meet face to face the truth is apt to be told on both sides. Wilson, after weighing the matter thoroughly, offered him the appointment of Secretary of State; but he did it with such candour, and Bryan accepted it with such generosity, that from that time each held the other's character in deep respect, though each watched the working of the other's mind a little dubiously. Wilson's leadership was at once established, and in matters where Bryan would have been at sea Wilson became practically his own Secretary of State. And Bryan's loyal coöperation made it possible to secure the support of Congress. Colonel House, who had been in constant consultation with Wilson, drew a breath of relief when the matter was settled.

Tumulty was appointed private secretary without need of consideration; he had served him satisfactorily in that capacity during his governorship, and Wilson liked him. The usual groans followed every appointment; this time it was Tumulty's religion. He was a Roman Catholic. Wilson at once made it clear, as he had always done, that a man's religion was his own affair, provided he was religious. This very question had come up once before when, as a law student at the University of Virginia, he had in a debate taken the stand that Catholicism was not dangerous to America; that he lost the debate did not alter his opinion. At Princeton he had taken exception to Dean West's prejudice against introducing a Unitarian into the faculty. Now Bryan was to be aghast at his liberality towards Unitarianism when he longed to have Eliot of Harvard in his Cabinet. Then Brandeis, whom he admired greatly, was a Jew — " And a fine one," Wilson retorted angrily when this objection was presented to him. It is singular that with so marked an attitude towards theological liberty, his " rigid Presbyterianism " is persistently emphasized. He was satisfied with his creed for himself, but religion meant to him the breath of God over His whole creation.

House was offered a position in the Cabinet but would not accept. He preferred to be the unofficial eyes and ears of the President, a position that apparently will never cease to be talked about. It was perhaps something amateurish in officialdom. However, people like a mystery. Simple as the relationship was, it will always be misconstrued.

Wilson's Cabinet was on the whole an efficient one, made up of men desirous of doing their best for the country. This, too, may be said about it: later, when its bitter enemies tried to find some evidence of corruption or dishonesty in its administration, they, with all their worst intentions on the alert, were baffled; they could fasten no material fault upon it, and all its members went out of office with a clean bill of political health.

VII

LEADER AND SERVANT OF THE PEOPLE

We dare not turn from the principle that morality and not expediency is the thing that must guide us and that we will never condone iniquity because it is most convenient to do so.

Woodrow Wilson

Chapter Seven

LEADER AND SERVANT OF THE PEOPLE

ON March 4, 1913, surrounded by the immense crowd usual on such occasions, Woodrow Wilson, on the rostrum before the Capitol, took his oath of office and made a short address. Both were done with an intensity of idealism that, while a good omen for the country, boded ill for his future happiness.

When the speaking and shouting were over the new President was driven to the White House where, from a platform, he was to review the army, the navy and the States' militia. Sitting near him I noticed afresh the gentle, courteous thought for those he loved that was always present with him, and the forgetfulness of self when another was in need. In the crowd as he looked down upon it, was a lame woman working her way with some difficulty to her place. He leaned over, evidently intent upon how he could help her. Fortunately some one in the crowd went to her assistance and the President's face lighted with a smile of relief.

After the roadway was cleared of the surging crowds, the broad avenue, empty and silent, seemed to stretch endlessly on. It was banked on either side by tiers of seats, hidden in green and flowers, where every State had its section marked by its own emblems. Then in the distance the procession moved up, first the army and the navy, then the States, each led by its Governor on horseback followed by his chief officials and the State militia. State after State took up its own story and song. As they passed the President's stand the Governors lifted their hats in a sweeping salute which he acknowledged with a bow; but his hat was off only to the country's flag and when a band played the national anthem. The hurly-burly of partisan politics was for the moment laid aside. This represented the country's ideal, strong, dignified, united; yet each State, with pride, keeping its own traditions and individuality. We were witnessing an impersonation of the motto of the United States: *E pluribus unum.* Wilson's face, as he watched, became an almost tragic mask of passionate purpose.

A man of great personal dignity and seriousness of character faces no light ordeal when he undertakes to be President of the United States. Privacy for him is at an end. From the time that he opens his eyes in the morning until he closes them at night he is under close observation; not from altruistic but purely from financial reasons — to help sell the daily papers by giving them items interesting to the taste of the masses. All this is a constant irritation, but the serious thing is that the incessant demands upon his time make thinking, before he acts on important matters, almost a juggler's feat.

Wilson knew exactly what he wanted and why he wanted it, and he believed that the country in electing him was sympathetic to his policies. He came to the presidency better equipped for the country's service than any President since the early days of the Republic. His promises to the people during his campaign were not the quick seizing of straws that might give him a momentary strategic position, but were convictions drawn from a life's study.

When he spoke his first message to Congress his suggestions for lowering the tariff were in working form.

At the first official meeting of his Cabinet on March 6th, when the members had taken their seats, Wilson said quietly, " Gentlemen, I shall have to give my attention to the graver problems of the Nation, and I shall not have time to see swarms of people who want office. I shall have to ask you to sift the applicants for me and to make your recommendations. I think I owe this to the people." So, quite casually, a long-accustomed habit was discarded. Since Jackson's day the Presidents had spent much of their time during the first year or more of office in distributing patronage; consequently the public business had suffered in efficiency and dignity, to say nothing of morality. Wilson swept away this precedent as a matter of course. After the first moment of astonishment the members of the Cabinet realized that in lifting his own office to its proper plane the President had increased the prestige of theirs. In the public eye the heads of the departments would be held to a greater responsibility and their influence with Congress strengthened.

Later during the meeting, Burleson, the Postmaster-General, said, " Mr. President, I shall not present anybody who fought you." The President quickly replied, " It makes no difference whether a man stood for me or not. All I want is a man who is fit for the place, a man who stands for clean government and progressive policies." There was another moment of astonishment. Good old Bryan was aghast; souls have different patterns and the spoils system was dear to his. Unfortunately, to pay the piper was such an integral part of the political custom of the day that a major operation was practically impossible; it would mean the death of the party. Wilson, no matter what he said of the beauty of compromise, hated it with a passion; now he was forced into it more or less. Nevertheless, he made a valiant fight; and throughout his administration, the whole trend of politics was upward.

From all accounts, a curiously friendly atmosphere was brought about in this first official cabinet meeting. One sees Bryan, the Secretary of State, fairly shedding a glow over his chief as he sat beaming beatitudes by his side. And though Bryan was biding his time soothingly to insinuate into the President's ear the justice of paying the men who had worked for him in the coin they wanted, and though Burleson knew that compromise would have to be made, Wilson's leadership was established and was acceptable to all.

A problem left over by the previous administration was the so-called " Six Power Loan " to China. Participation in this loan by New York bankers had been favourably viewed by Taft's Attorney-General. The loan was to be guaranteed by the several governments involved. If China failed to meet her indebtedness it might mean forcible intervention by the Powers, a situation Wilson would not contemplate for a moment. He promptly refused his support and the American bankers withdrew. It caused great enthusiasm in the country, but led to some consternation since the President gave his reply to the press before conferring with the diplomatic corps. One wonders where Colonel House was at the time.

Wilson's immediate task was that of making necessary appointments. One of the first was to appoint as medical adviser at the White House Lieutenant, later Admiral, Cary Grayson, a young medical officer in the navy, for whom he took an instant liking. From this time on Lieutenant Grayson was an intimate member of the official household, and was in close and constant attendance upon the President until his death.

Other and less personal appointments had to be made and, as with his cabinet, he had to meet many disappointments. The selection of acceptable ambassadors and ministers is made extremely difficult because of America's idea that high salaries paid to diplomats are inconsistent with American traditions. Yet the government knows that none but a rich man can afford to take such a post unless some private citizen helps him out. After failing to secure Dean Fine of Princeton as ambassador to Germany, and President Eliot of Harvard for England, he did secure Walter Hines Page for England, but was able to keep him there only by the generosity of his friend, Cleveland Dodge, who added $25,000 a year to what the government provided. It takes a good deal of patriotism for a man to pay out of his private purse the government's unquestioned obligations. There is neither sense nor justice in the practice; but that is the situation Wilson had to meet. He was unhappy enough over the matter and spoke of the pity that the country "had to ask sacrifices of those who are invited to serve it abroad, a service which every year becomes more exacting and more important."

The list of ministers and ambassadors finally selected contained a number of names Americans are proud to remember: Walter Hines Page's equal would be hard to find; Henry van Dyke and Thomas Nelson Page could speak English even to a Britisher's satisfaction; then there was Gerard at Berlin, and Brand Whitlock in Belgium, and Morgenthau at Constantinople. They were perhaps better equipped for peace than for war, but at the time of their taking office peace reforms were absorbing the world, and though Wilson was a detective story fan he ignored the prophecies of the immortal Oppenheim. Even the belligerent Roosevelt had won a peace prize and in the Democratic camp Bryan was mapping out a peace chart for the entire world. Carnegie had built his Peace Palace; the Kaiser was pouring out peaceful slogans. It seemed a perfectly reasonable time to make ambassadors of poets, novelists and historians. But what was curious was that all the peace propaganda was not merely the enthusiasm of the moment. We were living, at the breaking out of the Great War, in what was in reality not a military age. Poetry, the index finger of the time, was altruistic; there was not produced one single poem of note that glorified war. Kipling, before the Boer war came, wrote his great " Recessional "; and, when we breezed off to Cuba, Roosevelt and his Rough Riders figured more largely in caricature than in verse. The country adored Roosevelt and loved to see him romp around—even to the extent of a fight or two; but that was all. Wilson in his attitude was the real exponent of the temper of an age upon which broke the most disastrous war in centuries.

The business of selecting his ambassadors and ministers settled, the questions of reducing the tariff and the reform of the currency were of first consequence to him; for the early months of his administration were not only packed with the usual obstacles that meet the reformer, but there began ominous threatenings of storms from foreign countries. Wilson's attitude was somewhat that of a dictator; in foreign affairs it was his duty to be such, and he was clearly within his rights. His position towards the rights of other nations was so fixed that he apparently often acted without giving the questions that arose a thought; for he had clear fundamental ideas on which all his policies were founded. Mexico, Japan, the Panama Canal Zone, China

The G. O. P. Campaigners.

By permission of The Sun, *Baltimore, Md., and Mr. McKee Barclay*

"Now just look what *you* done!"

— there was but one attitude possible — hands off your neighbour's property. Nevertheless, though his actions were right and his cabinet was behind him and the country applauded, it might have been better if he had followed precedent and informed the State Department and the Diplomatic Corps of his decisions before giving them to the press. It took time and bitter experience for him to slacken the stride so successfully taken when Governor of New Jersey, and it is perhaps questionable whether he should have slackened it even to the extent he did. A man possessed with a demon for what he believes a righteous cause has to run his own course. He might have been a greater diplomat by compromising but he would not have been a greater man.

The day after the inauguration, in addition to the Mexican situation and the Chinese Loan, there was handed to Wilson on a very hot platter the serious dispute between the Pacific States (California and Washington) and Japan. These States had always been suspicious and afraid of the Japanese and did not want them in their territory under any circumstances. California particularly felt that the East had neither sympathy with, nor understanding of, her problem; she was entirely inconsiderate of the Federal Government and indifferent to diplomatic questions that might easily involve the country in a war. Japan, on her side, was incensed by the discrimination against her subjects, and sent a note to the United States that might easily have brought on a war. The situation was extremely critical and called for the most astute diplomacy. Wilson handled it in exactly the right way. He sent Bryan out to California to urge moderation and succeeded, through Bryan and the State Department, in appeasing the natural indignation of the Japanese. The question was still unsettled, though not in a menacing state, when the World War broke out and turned the thoughts of all away from it to that great conflagration.

There were other questions that could not be settled off hand. Two weeks before his inauguration Huerta had murdered Madero, President of Mexico, and usurped his power. Revolution was general throughout Mexico. Important American business interests had invested large sums in that country in mines, railroads, oil wells, and they urged armed intervention to protect their properties. This Wilson refused to supply, but he would not recognize a murderer; Huerta must go and a constitutional government be formed. He took firmly the stand that in the Latin-American countries the United States was not a bird of prey under cover of the Monroe Doctrine. Americans who went to these countries in order to make fortunes for themselves would not have the armed assistance of the United States; if they got into trouble they would have to abide by the laws of the countries they were in and settle their affairs in the local courts. The army and navy of the United States were not to be used for the benefit of fortune hunters. In his address at Mobile, October 27, 1913, on the *New Latin-American Policy*, he said, " I want to take this opportunity to say that the United States will never again seek one additional foot of territory by conquest." His address is infinitely sad in the light of the present, it is so full of an almost triumphant certainty that justice, mercy, truth must prevail. Throughout the speech too one feels his passion for the rights of the defrauded people.

He adopted a policy, which he called " watchful waiting," that nearly drove the militarists, and those anxious about their oil lands, frantic. The Mexicans, whom he wanted to help, were unimpressed. They had every reason to distrust the United States; they had been robbed and exploited by that country with the gusto of a mediaeval baron. They were used to Christian words and heathen deeds from their big neighbour; and they thought that "wary watching" was a wise slogan for them. Wilson's sympathy was all with the Mexicans. He felt that what was influencing the United States and other interested countries was merely their own advantage; that it was just "dollar diplomacy." He said at Mobile, "I have to pause and remind myself that I am President of the United States and not of a small group of Americans with vested interests in Mexico." To the Mexicans Wilson seemed to be playing for time, and they feared that, sooner or later, they would be annexed to the United States.

After various developments and when things were looking dubious, Wilson was compelled to occupy Vera Cruz. Then indeed the Mexicans were certain that the United States was not altruistic but was seeking her own interests. At the critical moment the A. B. C. Powers of South America offered their good offices to mediate. Wilson accepted instantly and threw the entire situation into the hands of these Powers. The change of feeling throughout Latin America was very dramatic. Convinced now that the President had meant every word he had said, that he had not the slightest desire for anything that was theirs but wanted only their good, a blaze of enthusiasm burst out for him. American flags were displayed in many countries. Though the questions in dispute were far from settled, an entirely different feeling was created between the United States and the Latin republics. If Wilson had been intimidated, hurried or persuaded to go to war with Mexico, the United States would have found herself a few years later in a more bewildering maze than she did.

There have been many different opinions about Wilson's Mexican policy. His own view is shown in his address to Congress in 1915, in which he said: " Whether we have benefited Mexico by the course we have pursued remains to be seen. Her fortunes are in her hands. We have shown that we will not take advantage of her in her distress."

From a long letter to Colonel House, dated June, 1916, I make the following extract:

" The break seems to have come in Mexico; and all my patience to have gone for nothing. I am infinitely sad about it. I fear I should have drawn Pershing and his command northward just after it became evident that Villa had slipped through his fingers; but except for that error of judgment (if it was an error) I cannot, in looking back, see where I could have done differently, holding sacred the convictions I hold in this matter.

" Right or wrong, however, the extremest consequences seem upon us. But *Intervention* (that is the rearrangement and control of Mexico's domestic affairs by the U. S.) there shall not be either now or at any other time if I can prevent it."

But the Mexican imbroglio was not quickly settled; it ran its troublous way through the eight years of Wilson's administrations.

Among the most important of Wilson's achievements were the reductions of the tariff and the establishment of the Federal Reserve Banks. On April 8, 1913, he delivered in person his message to Congress on the tariff. This method of communication with Congress had been obsolete since the days of Jefferson. Wilson revived it to foster a more intimate connection between the executive and legislative branches of the government; and it emphasized his conviction that the President should be the leader of the government. For a man who was not at all dramatic he produced a very dramatic effect. The House was packed with people, distinguished and otherwise, all more curious than enthusiastic. When the President entered the House rose and applauded. It is quite certain that if they had kept their seats, so intent was he on the message he was about to read and the desire to establish sympathetic relations with Congress, he would not have noticed it. After the House was again seated the Speaker said, "I have the distinguished honour of introducing the President of the United States." The President rose, bowed, and smiled unmistakably to his wife, who sat in the gallery, very pale and very proud.

The President's address was short and simple — and from the first the audience was his. After expressing his desire for intimate relations with Congress, avoiding all details, he presented a very general argument for reducing the tariff. He noted that the existing tariff was no longer the moderate protective tariff of the early days of the country; it had become merely a means of granting special favours to a privileged few and should be so altered as to open equal opportunities to all. The tariff should not be radically lowered at once; that would destroy business; it should be gradually lowered to allow business to adjust itself. The message was merely a short epitome of his article on *The Tariff Make-Believe* in the *North American Review* in 1909. It was easy to see, from the reception of his message, that his troubles with Congress would be negligible; and the *Underwood Tariff Bill*, embodying his ideas, passed the House in short time. But the Senate was another matter; there he was hotly pressed. A powerful lobby, working in the interest of protected industries, fought shamelessly. It became a scandal, and the President wrote to the papers a short note — so effective that it broke up the lobby. After that his success with the Senate was assured and the bill became law in September. It took four months of strenuous work by the President and the Democratic leaders in the Senate to accomplish this. It was his first official act to abolish special privilege.

When the tariff had practically been taken out of politics Wilson carried his point for a graduated income tax, to be levied according to the ability of the people to pay. This bill became law at the same time as the tariff bill. Summer in Washington to the Congressmen sweating over the reform bills, seemed bad enough to satisfy most of the reformers. It seemed to them only reasonable to relax a little and go fishing in a cooler climate. But their chief was inexorable: the currency bill must be enacted while the fire was hot. Under date of August 15, 1913, Mr. Wilson wrote:

> "The days go hard with me just now. I am alone. My dear ones went away almost at my command. I could not have been easy about them had they not gone; and we have found a nest for them in New Hampshire . . . which is ideal. . . . And so my mind is at ease about them. And yet, oh! the difference to me! It makes the situation complete, however, I must admit. These are stern days, and this all but empty house fits well with them. My secretary is living with me and the young naval doctor who is on my staff; and they are lovely fellows, both of them, and good company all the while. They are no substitutes, but in themselves most satisfactory. I work hard, of course (the amount of work a president is expected to do is preposterous), but it is not that that tells on a fellow. It's the anxiety attending the handling such "things" as that fellow Huerta and all other affairs

in which you seem to be touching quicksilver, matters for which your own judgments and principles furnish no standards, and with regard to which you can only frame conjectures and entertain hopes. I play golf every afternoon, because while you are playing golf you *cannot* worry and be preoccupied with affairs. Each stroke requires your whole attention and seems the most important thing in life. I can by that means get perfect diversion of my thoughts for an hour or so at the same time that I am breathing the pure out-of-doors. And I take Saturdays off, as nearly as may be when a telegram or a piece of news may waylay you and hold you up at any moment. Even Sundays are not safe. On the whole, however, I have myself well in hand. I find that I am often cooler in my mind than some of those about me. And I of course find a real zest in it all. Hard as it is to nurse Congress along and stand ready to play a part of guidance in anything that turns up, great or small, it is all part of something infinitely great and worth while, and I am content to labour at it to the finish. I keep perfectly well. My young aide looks after me as a mother would look after a child, and is with me practically all the time. So far things go very well, and my leadership is most loyally and graciously accepted, even by men of whom I did not expect it. I hope that this is in part because they perceive that I am pursuing no private and selfish purposes of my own. How could a man do that with such responsibilities resting upon him! It is no credit to be sobered and moralized by a task like this! "

It is difficult to understand how he could prefer, as he surely did, to work on vital problems, with his family, friends and relatives, all in close juxtaposition. "The people I love disturb me! " he once exclaimed in amazed incredulity, when such a thing was intimated. " Dear me! Margaret's singing, Nell's laughter, Jessie's loveliness and serious questionings, Ellen's looking at me with wondering, almost protesting eyes, when she finds me with detective tales or when I recite many limericks at the very moment a committee on labour is due! I should starve without the people I love. No, my friend," he added, " I need my family and I need my friends at all times. And though I may not be able to have them at all times I badly want them. So don't ever take yourself off, feeling you are an interruption. The idea! " He laughed at its absurdity.

On October 8th he wrote:

" We have now to go through the same thing with the currency measure that we went through with the tariff measure, and of the two I think the currency measure rather the more important."

The speed of the pace he set for himself and his coworkers, and the tenacity with which he held to a policy once undertaken, brought quick and lasting results; but that a man should feel such strenuous service was its own reward and that he wanted nothing for himself was disconcerting to the politicians.

Wilson had long felt the need of a change in the banking and currency system and had begun conferences on the subject even before his inauguration. It had engaged the attention of earlier congresses, but no satisfactory legislation had been passed. The credit of the country was controlled by a group of New York bankers and they could direct the business of the country to their own advantage. They wanted to increase their power by a central bank which would also be under their control. This was the height of special privilege, a thing he loved to fight; and a banking bill must be constructed and passed that would defeat the financial plutocrats. His blood was up and so was that of the bankers; it was to be a fight to a finish on both sides. A system must be developed, Wilson felt, that would make credit, now concentrated in a few hands, available to all properly entitled to it. Carter Glass, Representative from Virginia, had been working over a bill that would somewhat meet the case, and, though greatly altered in form, it became the nucleus of the finally approved bill. In the final form of the bill the country was divided into twelve districts in each of which a Regional Reserve bank was located as a central bank to serve all banks in that district that should be members of the system. The Regional Reserve banks were to be subject to the Federal Reserve Board, consisting of the Secretary of the Treasury, the Controller of the Currency, and three other members appointed by the President. Currency notes were to be issued by the Treasury through the Reserve banks. They would be thoroughly protected even without the government's guarantee. It took a tremendous amount of work, principally by the President, Carter Glass, Senator Owen and Secretary McAdoo, to secure these provisions.

Bankers fought hard for a single central bank. When this could not be obtained they fought for banker representation on the Federal Reserve Board. A delegation visited Wilson and made strong arguments for their view. After listening patiently, Wilson said:

"Will one of you gentlemen tell me in what civilized country of the earth there are important government boards of control on which private interests are represented?" And he followed with:

"Which of you gentlemen thinks that the railroads should select members of the Interstate Commerce Commission? " There was nothing more to be said on the subject.

Bryan, reflecting the ideas of his following, wanted the currency notes, issued by the Treasury, to have the guarantee of the Government. He had been preaching this doctrine for decades. Glass was equally earnest in insisting that they should be only the obligations of the banks; and he ably argued at a conference with the President that this was correct banking and that the notes would be fully secured. Things came almost to an *impasse* until Wilson remarked to Glass, " Every word you say is true; the Government liability *is* a mere thought. And so, if we can hold to the substance of the thing and give the other fellow the shadow, why not do it, if thereby we may save our bill? " Glass accepted this suggestion; and the Government guarantee gave to the great mass of the people, unfamiliar with fundamental banking principles, complete confidence in the security of the currency. Bryan was delighted, and through his influence many necessary votes were secured and the bill was passed by the House. It had rough going in the Senate but finally passed that body and became law when signed by the President on December 23, 1913.

Before the bill was presented to the House in June, 1913, the President appeared before Congress for the second time and made a short address, explaining the general purpose of the bill. " We must have a currency, not rigid as now, but readily, elastically responsive to sound credit, the expanding and contracting credits of every day transactions, the normal ebb and flow of personal and corporate dealings. Our banking laws must mobilize reserves; must not permit the concentration anywhere in a few hands of the monetary resources of the country or their use for speculative purposes in such volume as to hinder or impede or stand in the way of banking and of issue which our new laws are to set up; must be public, not private, must be vested in the Government itself, so that the banks may be the instruments, not the masters, of business and of individual enterprise and initiative."

It took time and much hard work to organize and establish the regional banks. They were opened in midsummer, 1914. The new system was of inestimable benefit to the country. The strain thrown on the finances of the country by the Great War was satisfactorily met. It is appalling to think of what would have happened if the old system had still been in force.

There has been much discussion as to who contributed most to the character of this law. When we remember that Wilson had studied the financial system of the country for many years and that he had a remarkable grasp of the fundamental problem, in spite of his joking remark that he knew nothing of banking, and that he made the final decision on every detail of the bill, we are led to agree with Carter Glass when he said: "The serious fact is that the master-mind of the whole performance was Woodrow's. It was his infinite prescience and patience; it was his courage and wisdom; it was his patriotism and power — his passion to serve mankind — that gave zest and inspiration to the battle for financial freedom."

There were a few men around the President like Glass, not in the least desirous of saying, "I did it," and who were absorbed in national problems and not in themselves, but there were very few. It would be absurd to discuss the question of who deserves credit for many of his successful reforms, except that so many claims have been made by the reminiscence writers of that period. A deluge of memoirs followed the war; politicians, scholars, poets, novelists, all concentrated upon the figure of Wilson, enlarging, distorting, never portraying the man as he was, most fearful lest a great light might eclipse their little flicker. The times were so fateful, so terrible, that any one having a part in them saw things out of focus. He is reported to have said humourously, "I really thought of some of these things myself."

The Mexican policy, the tariff reform, the currency reforms, the trust laws, the Chinese loan decision, and the Panama tolls question, these, settled by him in the first two years of his administration, are stamped all over with his mind and purpose. Special privilege, the exploiting of one class for the benefit of another, he would prevent if he could. Perhaps the dominant keynote of his life was his conception of justice. "Give me justice and I will take care of myself," he said when a young man in Georgia. "The poor boy must have the same right at the University that the rich boy has," he said when at Princeton. "The people of New Jersey shall not be cheated by the bosses," he said when Governor of New Jersey. "Justice, and only justice, shall always be our motto," he said in his first presidential inaugural address. This definite attitude simplified matters, for, where principles were involved, all argument was eliminated. Such singleness of purpose had naturally its annoying side to any politician given to whipping the devil around the post.

On March 4, 1914, President Wilson ended his first year in office. Frank Cobb, of the *New York World*, wrote: "It has been a year of achievement for which there are few, if any, parallels in American history." After summing the year's work he places as highest of all "the restoration of responsible representative government on the fundamental principles of the party. That is the great fruit of his leadership. He has done it, not by the bribery of the patronage; not by denunciation and intrigue and chicanery; not by selling one promise in order to buy the fulfillment of another promise; but by mere intellectual and moral domination, the only kind of leadership that does not lead to disaster. The influence that he exercises over Congress and his party is not the influence of a chief executive clothed with far-reaching legal powers, but it is the influence of a trained and disciplined mind backed by sincerity and purpose. That is the noblest form of leadership that a democracy can produce.

In his inaugural address Mr. Wilson said: "This is not a day of triumph; it is a day of dedication." Even the strongest opponent of his policies cannot impeach that pledge. The President has kept the faith. Under his leadership his party has kept the faith. That is the supreme vindication of American institutions. Everything else depends on the fitness of the people themselves for self-government and for the responsibilities of self-government.

Former President Taft wrote: "It is a real satisfaction to one who knows the atmosphere of Washington to note the success of a strong character in dealing with a situation and improving the opportunity it offers. . . . I rejoice in the existence of a situation in which the party in power is fulfilling its promises made in the platform, and is doing so by following the guidance of the head of the party, who is charged by the people with the party's responsibility." Such a generous tribute to a successful opponent has permanency.

VIII
STORM SIGNALS

An Ideal is only a flaming reality.
Conrad

Chapter Eight

STORM SIGNALS

WILSON's life would have exhausted itself long before it did except for the beauty and peace that came to him from his family relationships and his close and dear friendships. No matter what storms were brewing in the nation there was rarely a moment when his friends could not reach him. A young Englishman, a conservative member of Parliament, was visiting in America a friend of the President. "Do you think your President is a little inclined to radicalism?" he asked his hostess. "Would you like to meet him?" she answered. "If so, I shall see if he can have us to lunch or tea." "But," answered the Englishman, shocked, "I shouldn't, you know, do that; it would be most extraordinary." "I am sure the President would not think it so," his hostess laughed. "You see, he happens to be my friend, and his friends count more with him than friends do with most people. Wait and see." She telegraphed and a reply came at once. "Delighted. Come over to lunch tomorrow at one. Bring whom you will." The Englishman looked serious; he was not in the least enamoured of democracy. He hesitated, but decided to risk the situation. He intimated that an American might not consider an invitation from the President really an order, but of course it was. When they reached the White House the next morning they were, in the least possible time, ushered into a room where, in beautiful, dignified surroundings, the President and his family were waiting. The President was, of course, simple and unaffected. As the Englishman said later, there was something about him unforgettable, something that stamps the face of those who are accustomed to lead and who habitually live with the highest in thought and spirit. At lunch the talk was of the lightest, mostly of who were the best detective story writers and how grave was the crime of authors who dared to lead you on with false clues. A few good limericks had been recited, and Wilson remarked how delightful it was just to laugh. Suddenly, without warning, he turned upon the Englishman, who was busy making mental notes, and said, "What are you Englishmen thinking of, letting the Irish go on as they are doing? Now I would just send an army over and stop it all if I were King." The Englishman gasped and one of the group said, "Oh, would you, O Emperor? How about Mexico?" The President laughed and said, "Now, that's business; this is just talking." Then his face became very grave. "That scoundrel, Huerta!" he exclaimed. As they drove home the Englishman said, "He is the greatest man I ever saw. But why? He was only in a light mood and terribly imprudent, talked in such a way that a malicious person might give his words without his meaning and make a lot of mischief." "That is very characteristic of the President," was the answer. "He has no prudence at all in the midst of his friends and with his family. And the fact that any one is brought into his circle by one of his friends for social purposes would be a guarantee to him that he was a gentleman. For a man to accept his hospitality and betray his host would of course mean that he was a spy, not a gentleman. That is the very simple way he looks at life — and sometimes regrets it."

There is a stratum that runs through the world quite

free from alloy; it is the highest that civilization reaches; there live the men and women who have no need of pretence, for they are the thing they seem to be. They can be kind without thought that they are conferring a favour; they need no badge to augment their self respect, or any other person to bolster up their importance. They are free and unafraid. In that class were Woodrow Wilson and his wife, a class rather puzzling to many officials in Washington.

The splendid work Wilson was doing would not have been possible if he had allowed his time, his thoughts, to be disturbed by official social functions; ever present in his mind during the presidential years was the thought: " I am the servant of the people." And he often said, " My time of service is short. I must keep to essentials." As a matter of fact his natural taste was to keep aloof from the diplomatic balls; the how-do-you-do and how-do-you-do again side of life was distasteful to him. Colonel House greatly relieved him in such matters, attending to the demands of the dignitaries and diplomats.

The President was intensely grateful to him. He could never believe that, in being so useful, the Colonel was not sacrificing himself with complete disinterestedness upon the altar of friendship and his country's service. Now and then when any one ventured to be so brave as to suggest that the Colonel was having a grand time and that the rôle of American Prime Minister had its allurements, the President was so cold to what he thought such silly chatter that there was no encouragement for mischief-makers.

It would have been impossible to introduce any gossip that was not good-humoured into the President's home. In those happy days, before the marriages of his two daughters and Mrs. Wilson's death, it was a most delightful household — laughter, music, the best of talk — how generous they were in thought and deed! Any one of them would have shared her last crust with a friend — indeed, the danger would have been that the friend would have got the whole crust.

Jessie, the second daughter, was married eight months after her father's inauguration to Francis Sayre of Boston; the members of the family were very happy about it. "He is almost good enough for Jessie," the President said. One remembers the wedding at the White House when the watchman on the tower might easily have predicted all fair ahead for this gentle family that only longed to give to, not to take from, life. Six months later, Eleanor, the youngest daughter, married William Gibbs McAdoo, Secretary of the Treasury. The wedding was very quiet as Mrs. Wilson was far from well. She was the first person in the world to her husband. He did not see that upon her brow was the broad arrow and that very near indeed she was to journey's end. Into neither had entered any definite fear; she was only tired, they thought. Life was thrilling to her. How she rejoiced as he put over one piece of constructive work after another! It seemed to them both the beginning of what he could and would do for the nation.

Colonel House had gone to Europe in May, 1914, at the request of the President, who felt that the attitude of foreign countries in regard to Mexico and other international matters was confusing and could be better understood by direct approach. For such a mission his friend seemed almost ideal. Colonel House could always talk with a fool and not seem irritated; he could talk with a villain and not be shocked; and he could talk with a prime minister or a king and be tactful enough to make him unbosom his thoughts. These accomplishments the President felt that he himself sorely lacked. He showed irritation when talking with a fool; he could not be on easy terms with a villain, not to save any situation; and he could never feel that position made a man important. It was a great relief to have some one who could supplement these defects. The President knew exactly what he wanted and Colonel House's mission was not so naïve as it seemed. He and the President, in secret conclave concocting a European scheme, were doing very much what the world has been experimenting with for some years past. The Colonel and the President were just a trifle ultra-modern. Added to this was a touch of originality in Colonel House's lack of official position. The Colonel undertook the mission with the keenest pleasure. In his *Intimate Papers* his editor writes:

"Thus Colonel House set forth on his extraordinary mission, a private American citizen whose only relevant title was 'personal friend of the President', a single individual hoping to pull the lever of common sense that might divert the nations of the Old World from the track of war to that of peace. To inject himself successfully into the core of the European maelstrom demanded as much courage as diplomatic deftness. These qualities he possessed, as well as a sense of proportion which caused him often to laugh at the stark humour of the odds against him. But the stake for which he played was tremendous. It was the peace of the world. If he failed no harm was done. And if he succeeded. . . .

"He called his mission the Great Adventure."

The adventuring Colonel had an interview with the Kaiser and other lesser notables in Berlin; and in England he reached the ear of Lord Grey. It all sounds like a chapter out of an Oppenheim mystery tale, where kings, prime ministers, and such-like are our boon companions. It must have been heartening to believe that there were no villains for whom we were responsible, not one. They were all from Germany and Mexico. We wanted nothing at all for ourselves — only to change the character of the world!

The President's letters to Colonel House show that if the Colonel was delighted to undertake the responsibility of an international psychological interpreter, the President was equally delighted to have him do so, and was more than satisfied with his methods. A letter dated July 16, 1914, shows how he felt. The letter begins, "My dear friend." The President then expresses pleasure at receiving Colonel House's letter, written from Paris just after his visit to Berlin. He feels that House has begun a great mission and rejoices over it, that he is doing it in just the right way with characteristic tact and quietness; he feels that he could not himself have done the thing nearly so well. He signs himself, "With sincere affection, Faithfully, Woodrow Wilson."

Colonel House found matters in Europe alarming. He wrote Wilson from Berlin, "The situation is extraordinary. It is militarism run stark mad." That was on May 29, 1914. He was frightened, but not so much frightened as to feel that he might not possibly prevent war. The fuse had been burning a long time and was near its end, but few realized it except those actually involved.

Over Wilson's life until now there had been few storm signals. Now they began to come with rapid and terrific force. In the beginning of August, 1914, the European War broke out. The New York Stock Exchange closed its doors; Americans were stranded in Europe; there was a panic throughout the world.

Mrs. Wilson was desperately ill. For some time her condition had been growing more and more critical, and after many fluctuations of hope and fear she died on August 6th.

The little lady at the White House took with her on her last journey thankfulness for a reform she had been able to accomplish: she had hoped to hear before her death of the passage of a bill providing for better housing conditions of the poor in the crowded alleys of Washington. Congress, learning of her wish, acted quickly, and before unconsciousness came it was granted — very light baggage to carry with her " to that strand of the daughters of the sunset." Hers had never been a grasping hand; her little worldly possessions could not have caused envy to the poorest in the land. She slipped away without need of tearing up roots; death was for her a continuance of her real life which drew its being from Him who, she believed, was God. Mirage or substance, it was a powerful elixir. What was true of her was true of the man she loved. Had he died then, tragedy would have passed him by. The country grieved for him in his sorrow; and later some felt that the death of a mid-Victorian lady, so simple, so unobtrusive, was an international calamity. Many believed that he would not have gone to Europe nor have compromised with the Treaty had his first wife lived. Who knows? It is all guesswork; but we do know that he was influenced out of the ordinary by the people whom he loved and who were near him, invariably feeling that his ideals and theirs were the same. If his estimate were wrong, he could easily be put at a disadvantage. So long as his first wife lived there was perfect harmony of action and motive between them. His daughter, Margaret, writes: " Mother and father shared every great aim, were working to sacrifice all the things of this world for the things of the spirit. In fact, they were not conscious of sacrificing them, just letting them go because of a greater love."

After Mrs. Wilson's death Wilson's close relationships were with people of quite a different outlook. With them it was not so much a question of right or wrong; it was a question of values. What was wise and right in worldly, to him unessential, matters was wise and right and very essential to them. He had a great deal to give and to be that the world valued and he did not. The man was always loved by those about him, but his ideals were beyond most of us. His actions may have been influenced at a time when his every action affected the world though his purpose stood steadfast. The wisdom of his actions will always be debated but the integrity and wisdom of his purpose cannot be questioned. When he stood in the home of his boyhood, beside the grave of his wife, his mind swept back to the reconstruction period after the Civil War when they were both so determined to help with all their powers to rebuild a broken world. And were the years that had followed, so full of sane achievement, to be wiped out? Was it to be as though they had died in their youth — as though they had never been? Queer and unrelated thoughts rush over people in crises of sorrow. He left the spot determined that all his efforts should be given to keep his country out of war. Into this aim he would throw an immense patience and all the faith and intellect he possessed. He felt overwhelmingly that he was the custodian of his country's safety. He did not see that, as had been hitherto the history of his life, he was to take up almost alone the people's cause.

When the President returned to Washington after the burial of his wife in Georgia, he wrote to me that his loneliness was almost beyond his endurance, but, at least, Ellen was at rest. He had seen her suffer so much physically and her power of vicarious suffering was so great, a world at war would have broken her heart. His call to incessant action made it easier for him than it could possibly have been for her.

Behind Wilson lay his splendid civic achievements. He was esteemed, by virtue of his practical work and his comprehension of the science of government, one of the greatest of Democratic Presidents. Now he faced the avalanche of war and the problems of reconstruction. With impaired sight, hardened arteries and other physical ills, he faced the future, at 58, determined that all his efforts should be devoted to keeping his country out of the war.

In his official life he had no doubt of his own strength; there his self-confidence was enormous; he felt himself heart to heart with the people, and this belief fortified him against his opponents as nothing else could do. He was working for the people, not for himself.

At the onset of the war, when Germany without a scruple marched through Belgium, saying that it was a necessity of war and that treaties were mere scraps of paper, the President of the United States held his rage in check, and officially proclaimed the neutrality of the country. He knew the great varieties in our population and he was fearful of a divided people. In an appeal to the people he said: "Every man who really loves America will act and speak in the true spirit of impartiality and fairness and friendliness to all concerned. . . . The United States must be neutral in fact as well as in name during these days that are to try men's souls. We must be impartial in thought as well as in action. . . ."

It was shouted all over the world in derision that he had asked the country to be neutral in thought as in deed. He asked nothing so absurd; for to be neutral in thought would be not to think at all. But he did ask them to be " impartial," which meant the use of the highest type of intellect there is, that of the judge, not the advocate. Such an old, old story now; so worn with constant going over that it can hardly be deciphered! But then it set the emotions of the world aflame. The European nations at first undervalued the President's statesmanship. The words " pacifist " and " theorist " were much on their lips, but he was incapable of merciful muddling. With all his hatred of war, and his fair words, his eye was keenly on the lookout, his intellect intent on safeguarding his country. A historian, a statesman, a patriot was at the helm, a man who believed that reasonableness is the sanity of the mind.

The vast mass of Americans at first felt the United States a long way off from the European trouble; even those stranded in Europe could not conceive of such a catastrophe as their country being involved. One of our ministers who, one should suppose, might have known better, sent word to friends who were taking the last boat over to England that it was ridiculous to suppose that England was going to enter the war any more than we were. And England was declaring war even as he spoke.

Wilson, with most of the world, felt, in August, 1914, that the war would be over in six months, and that a great neutral country, able and ready to help, would be a broken world's greatest asset. But when trench warfare developed and no decisive advantage was gained by either side, he looked forward to a long struggle. The only hope of shortening the war seemed to him to be by appealing to the conscience of those in authority and to their intelligence and common sense. This he meant to try with all the influence he possessed.

After the first universal feeling that America's entry into the war was unthinkable, and the first sympathetic response to the President's messages and attitude, the wind changed, and he became the target of all the irresponsible prejudices let loose throughout the world. The propagandists honeycombed the land, instilling poison where they could. Violent, undigested opinions head-lined the papers — and steadily from the White House came the words "Think before you speak," an appeal to the God in man, to the conscience of the people. Looking upon the country always as a whole Wilson knew that, in spite of the fire of criticism from many directions, the temper of the people was with him. For fifteen years America had been bent on destroying autocracy; the country at large was not in sympathy with autocratic government. Nevertheless Wilson knew well the danger of clever unscrupulous men working upon ignorant people. He knew that the latter were inflammable material and that, unless he could counteract the work of the propagandists and educate the people through his notes and messages, there would be danger of a divided country. It was the same danger that we had incurred when, after the French Revolution, the pro-French Americans and pro-English Americans almost brought the country to disruption. If we had to enter the war, he was determined that we should do so only when the country was united by feeling as well as by necessity.

The large German population at home called for fine diplomacy on the President's part, and the pro-English were almost as difficult to handle, while the business interests utterly resented the English blockade. The Germans pamphleteered the country with indignant protests, claiming that the President was using mild words to the English while he was using threatening language to the Germans in regard to their submarines. He was harassed not only by these important elements of the nation, but the gamblers in stocks were adding their voices to the confusion of sounds. The President kept his head and his temper. He quietly pointed out the difference between interfering with commerce and destroying American lives.

His absorption in these great and pressing difficulties did not lessen his interest in individuals. An American holding a position of trust in Europe had fallen into habits which were giving rise to gossip and which might easily have affected his reputation for high morality in his own country. The situation was brought to the President's notice. He quietly called him back to America on some simple pretext, but in reality to give him, in his home surroundings, a chance to see his danger in perspective and to recover his natural poise. It worked wonderfully. A re-established man returned to his post entirely unaware, then or thereafter, that the President's finger had moved in his affairs. Many instances of this order might be given; for, though Wilson was not especially interested in redeeming sinners, he was very persistent in trying to prevent the waste of good material. He felt, in the words of Robert Bridges, that "Corruption of the best is ever the worst corruption."

Even in these strenuous days his instant attention to the smallest request of any friend was remarkable. At a time when he was especially busy, and very shortly before his second marriage, I wrote saying that I should like to see him for a few moments — nothing especially important or very personal. Instantly came the reply that Congressmen were rushing upon him from every quarter and it was difficult to call a moment his own. He wanted to run over to see me at once, but just could not manage it. "Congress meets tomorrow; Tuesday I must address it; Wednesday I am to entertain the Democratic National Committee at lunch." Couldn't I take lunch with him on Thursday and have a little talk afterwards?

A short time before I had asked him to try and obtain the release of a delicate English boy who was a prisoner in Germany. The answer under date July 5, 1915, was equally prompt and showed no annoyance:

"I do not know whether it will be possible to do anything for young B— in the present temper of the German government, but I am going to try. . . . I am writing to the Secretary of State about it today to get his advice."

He was successful in obtaining the boy's release.

I have many notes illustrating this characteristic of his friendship; and I am sure every friend of his could show just as many of the same kind. We could together compile a large, dull and convincing volume of inconsiderate requests from us and of overgenerous responses from him.

Every member of his family, every friend of his, felt at liberty to ask him for some trifling favour and, even though he might be on his way to an important Cabinet meeting, he would stop and consider it. But when it was a question of patronage he never allowed his feelings of friendship to interfere with what he considered his duty to the country. There was no nepotism during his administration.

As the burdens of his responsibilities grew ever heavier the loneliness in his home was, at least, lifted. His daughters and those near him were sympathetic when he became engaged to Mrs. Norman Galt, of Washington. They were married on December 18, 1915.

In a letter, referring to the expected happiness in his approaching marriage, he wrote: "The last fourteen months have seemed to me, in a world upset, like fourteen years. It is not the same world in which my dear Ellen lived." It was that amazing thing, a world thrown violently out of harmony with the spirit of the age. The President, determined to live in the spirit of the age, stood out as its spokesman with a certain solitary grandeur. He was grimly hopeful; surely humanity would come to its senses, would not throw off the hard-won fruits of civilization.

In his Cabinet, the Secretary of State, Bryan, was difficult to manage; and, although Wilson was practically his own Secretary of State, the official Secretary could not altogether be prevented from pouring too much soothing oil into wrong channels. There never was a more honest man than Bryan, but his mind was like what is commonly ascribed to women — intuitive, emotional — but, in logical reasoning, lacking. Garrison, Secretary of War, was not in accord with the President; in the matter of preparedness he wanted a large standing army; to this Wilson as well as Congress was entirely averse. On the other hand, McAdoo was an efficient Secretary of the Treasury; Burleson and Houston were both able men; Daniels, Secretary of the Navy, satisfied the President, though he satisfied few others; and Colonel House was always at hand with sympathy and practical help. Still, to be overtaken by such a storm, with his Secretary of State not to be depended upon and his Secretary of War at odds with his purposes, was not promising for peace of mind. But peace of mind was a thing of the past for him; and peace of conscience without it, is the martyr's reward. As the times grew sterner only a small handful of persons in high places stood by the President in his immense self-control. Day after day the papers reeked with denunciations by the martially minded, but he stoically closed his mind to their abuse and kept his ear to what he thought the heart of the country. To be, as Wilson felt himself to be, the mind and heart and soul articulate of the people, was a great and lonely task.

In his effort to comprehend the psychology of foreign nations through the medium of Colonel House, and have them understand him, the President continued to feel that the Colonel was his own personality at work in the foreign field; both had the same desires for peace — and for the same order of peace. As the *impasse* about neutral rights became more tangled, the President, early in 1915, asked the Colonel to undertake another visit to Europe to see what he could do to bring about a clearer understanding, taking as a foregone conclusion that all wanted peace. It was unfortunate that Wilson could not personally attend to these matters for he was particularly effective at first hand. When he addressed Congress in person and moved freely among congressmen and senators, he brought them to his way of thinking by the sheer force of his personality. His record in New Jersey tells the same story. A lifelong friend, who knew his power of personal appeal, used to say, whenever some one in the heat of partisan fury denounced the President, "Meet him and you will change your mind," and, indeed, the effect of seeing and talking to him was almost instantaneous, he was so lovable, so humorous, frank, and outspoken, so easy of approach, although never familiar. It was, however, impossible for him to be in Europe; consequently Colonel House's mission seemed imperative.

In the early months of 1915 a number of merchantmen had been attacked by German submarines and several Americans were lost. The culmination of this method of warfare was the torpedoing and sinking of the *Lusitania* on May 7, 1915, with the loss of one hundred and sixteen American lives.

A few days later the President addressed a group of foreign-born citizens in Philadelphia just after their naturalization ceremonies. He said, " There is such a thing as a man being too proud to fight. There is such a thing as a nation being so right that it does not need to convince others by force that it is right." He was not thinking of the *Lusitania*. He was placing before the new citizens an ideal of America, a country bent on progress by peaceful methods, too sure of its principles to " rattle the sabre." " Sure," he had said a few weeks earlier, " that when you are right you may be calm." But " too proud to fight " was an unfortunate phrase at that time; it was taken from its context, broadcast throughout the world, and given any interpretation that suited the mood of the interpreter. Even Colonel House and Ambassador Page, in Europe, worried over the effects of such inopportune words. Neither knew what the President would say next.

Then came the *Lusitania* note. In it Wilson firmly insisted on the rights of " American citizens bound on lawful errands as passengers on merchant ships of belligerent nationality," and repeated what he had said in a former note, that " This government must hold the Imperial German Government to a strict accountability for any infringement of these rights, intentional or incidental." He pointed out the " practical impossibility of employing submarines in the destruction of commerce without disregarding those rules of fairness, reason, justice and humanity which all modern opinion regards as imperative. . . .

" The Imperial German Government will not expect the Government of the United States to omit any word or act necessary to the performance of its sacred duty of maintaining the rights of the United States and its citizens and of safeguarding their free exercise and enjoyment."

The militarists shouted for immediate war, but the West was indifferent. Secretary Houston writes: " I was in the West for five weeks following this tragedy. I realized clearly then that the majority of the people were not even thinking of this nation's entering the struggle. I was in most parts of the Union several times between 1915 and the spring of 1917, and at no stage up to that time, were the masses of the people ready for this nation's participation."

Wilson, naturally impulsive, high-spirited and a fighter, forced his intellect to control his emotions. If an adverse fate should force us into the war, he was determined it should be with a united country. His determination to remain neutral as long as it was honourably possible was unchanged; the fusillade of attacks from the bellicose did not disturb him; but his friends as well as his enemies were disturbed, for the times were perilous and nerves everywhere tortured.

The note at once brought approval from all except the extreme militarists. Page, immensely relieved, cabled, " May I be allowed to express my personal satisfaction on the note? " and mentioned members of the British government as well as Landsdowne, Balfour and Bonar Law, as giving private expressions of praise. And in America Taft wrote that it was " admirable in tone, dignified in the level the writer takes with respect to international obligations; it may well call forth our earnest concurrence and confirmation."

Germany was evasive; and so Wilson's first note was followed by another and then another, each a forceful, convincing blow against her attitude, evincing a determination to make her account for her actions. And this at last he succeeded in doing. His third note ended with the warning that " repetition by commanders of German naval vessels of acts in contravention of those American rights must be regarded by the government of the United States, when they affect American citizens, as deliberately unfriendly." But Bryan was so fearful that the tone of the notes would lead to war in direct opposition to his pacifist principles, that he was unwilling to sign them as Secretary of State, and he therefore resigned before the second note was sent. It must be said to his credit that he was always a supporter of Wilson. Lansing was advanced to fill his place.

Conditions were becoming dangerous; neutrality was becoming difficult, and Wilson began a campaign for preparedness, increasing the army and the navy and developing means of making available the natural resources of the country. Yet he hoped until the very end that a peace might be brought about before we should be obliged to take part. Dr. Garfield wrote me that he said to him at this time, " We must keep ourselves in readiness to quench the fires of war." And to me Wilson said, " The outlook is very dubious; but I shall keep steering for peace; perhaps even a good peace may come if we are in earnest about it. The country looks to me to keep it out of war; and, God helping me, I will."

After the sinking of the *Arabic* in August, 1915, he sought Colonel House's advice in dealing with the affair. He wrote him on August 21st: " Two things are plain to me: First, the people of the country count on me to keep them out of war. Second, it would be a misfortune to the whole world if we should be drawn into the conflict, and so lose all disinterested influence over the final settlements." He thought that Walter Page " needs a bath in American opinions," but it is very useful " to have him give us the English view so straight."

Even before our entrance into the war Wilson's sympathies tallied largely with those of Page, but he kept them on ice. He was afraid that Page, so close to the tragedy, might lose control of his emotions; in his treatment of Page he was merely holding the lid down on his own as well as on Page's natural instincts.

There was little peace for the President. " Certainly this is a time when America expects every man to do his duty without thought of profit or advantage to himself." Such words, to many business men who were making large profits out of the war, were extremely irritating. Nevertheless he continued to say them, for he believed that " the opinion of the world is the mistress of the world." And it was that opinion he meant to try and influence for the only good he knew was worth considering — a moral good.

Along with this idealization he was never a dreamer. There is no doubt that he was a great preacher, but he was also a master workman. The laws that he forced, and those that he attempted to force through Congress, were remarkable; economists now agree on their sound common sense. Many remember the fight he and his Secretary of the Treasury made to create a large merchant marine. They hammered at Congress for years to secure a shipping bill to increase our ships. Less than a tenth part of the country's exports could be taken care of by American ships; and Britain's ships were being pressed more and more into war service. But Congress was stubborn, and it was not until 1919 that the bill was passed. The delay cost the country many millions of dollars. Another great reform that he had in view at the outset of his presidency was the Farm Loan Act. It was passed in 1916, and gave poor farmers the benefit of low rates of interest and long-term credits. With all its philanthropy it was sound business. Each step was contested by his enemies and he had to fight his way through every difficulty that could beset a man, in order to accomplish constructive work for the country as a whole. Hardly a day passed that the people did not see in their daily papers words of high idealization from their President. " Weasel words," his enemies shouted; but, to their amazement, the country thought otherwise.

Labour had organized and, with Gompers at its head, suddenly had the country by the throat. The Brotherhoods of Railway Engineers, Firemen, and Conductors declared that they would bring on a strike which would tie up every business in the country. It would unquestionably have given Germany a victory if they had carried out their threat and the strike had persisted for any length of time. The Railway Unions asked for an eight-hour day and the railway managers refused to grant the demand. The President proposed arbitration. Labour, knowing it had the whip-hand, refused. Wilson took the side of Labour, went before Congress and succeeded in having passed what was known as the Adamson law. It was a remarkable piece of quick, far-reaching legislation. The dispute between Government and Labour was ended. Wilson's sympathy was with Labour, but his action at this time was merely common-sense realization that work could not be halted at that moment without utterly disastrous results, that Labour's pistol was pointed at the head of the Government. What he did was to yield promptly and seek a law that would prevent such a thing from recurring.

Everything that envy and jealousy could contrive was done to break the President's morale, to destroy an influence that many could not comprehend. Mexico, with the aid of German propagandists, was making as much trouble as she could. The coming presidential election was causing the opposition to search their minds for every trick that could help their campaign — an interesting spectacle which recurs every four years.

But Wilson was a peculiarly aggravating creature. His enemies loathed his good qualities; nothing he did was right in some eyes; everything he did was super-right in others. Among the reasons for the clash of estimates were the marked individuality of his character and the invincibility of his ideals; right and wrong were so widely apart in his mind that there could be no compromise between them, and his conception of right and wrong was not open to argument. Many important men in the country, big business men, themselves accustomed to lead, who had held practically everything in their own hands — predatory wealth, as Roosevelt called them — hated him. He was working for the country, they for themselves. And the impetuous, among them some of the finest and noblest men in the country, were infuriated by sermons when they wanted action. The world was like a mammoth auditorium ablaze, and the task was to keep the people from trampling on each other.

Early in 1916 a difference developed between the President and Secretary of War Garrison. Garrison wanted a large permanent army maintained by conscription. The President wanted a moderate increase of the regular army and a volunteer citizens' army of four hundred thousand to be given a limited amount of training and to form the nucleus of a large army if occasion should make it necessary. This difference of opinion led to Garrison's resignation. Early in March Newton D. Baker was appointed Secretary of War.

The Republican forces had been lining up for the presidential election of 1916. Hughes had been nominated for the presidency and Wilson felt it extremely dubious whether he would be re-elected. Colonel House shared this uncertainty and wrote to the President: " If Hughes is elected — which God forbid — what do you think of asking both Lansing and Marshal to resign, appoint Hughes Secretary of State, and then resign yourself? This would be a patriotic thing to do. . . . Such a procedure would save the situation from danger and embarrassment. . . ."

This plan fully met with the President's approval, as it was in line with his lifetime views on the subject.

The returns of the election of November 7th sent the country to bed with the conviction that Hughes had been elected. In the morning, to every one's astonishment, fuller returns showed that Wilson had received a majority of nearly six hundred thousand votes. It was the South and West that had elected him because he had kept the country out of war — a very striking reminder to the East that if war had been declared at the time of the sinking of the *Lusitania* the country would not have been behind the President.

A few days later the President wrote me, " Strange as it may seem, I went to bed that night feeling a great burden lifted. . . . Now the burden upon me is heavier than ever. If we can escape entering the war and bring about a rational peace, it is something worth living and dying for, and I believe the country feels that way or it would not have re-elected me."

It was in this temper of mind that his second term began.

IX
THE UNITED STATES AT WAR

. . . there ever rolls
A vast idea before me, and I glean
Therefrom my liberty. . . .

Keats

Chapter Nine

THE UNITED STATES AT WAR

WILSON'S re-election for a second term was not, to some of his friends, cause for rejoicing. The last years of his first term had been years of unprecedented strain; and the storm ahead, they knew, would be met with an intensity of selfless purpose.

"The unconquerable will
And courage never to submit or yield"

were his. The air was ominous of tragedy, with his figure in the centre. Tragedy should be seen in dramatic representation or when the tragic hero has become a legend. In real life she loses her gorgeousness and her sceptered pall. From the beginning of his second term until his death Wilson was seen and recognized by all the world to be fighting a tragic fight for an ideal. That fight cannot be forgotten for it is typical of the eternal struggle of civilization against barbarism. It is to save Wilson's share in that struggle that the story of his life has been told and retold.

In the autumn of 1916 matters were reaching a climax; and Wilson's attitude was something like that of a physician who fears that his patient is near death yet keeps working on until the last breath is drawn.

In December the Germans asked for a conference with the Entente Powers to arrange a peace, with the evident intention of basing it on their occupation of enemy territory. This the Entente rejected.

Wilson, who was kept well informed of the undercurrents by Colonel House and Ambassador Gerard, had been contemplating a move towards peace. Within a few days of the receipt of the German proposals he sent notes to all the belligerents asking their views " as to the terms upon which the war might be concluded and the arrangements which would be deemed satisfactory as a guaranty against its renewal or the kindling of any similar conflict in the future as would make it possible frankly to compare them. . . . He [the President] takes the liberty of calling attention to the fact that the objects, which the statesmen of the belligerents on both sides have in mind in this war, are virtually the same, as stated in general terms to their own people and to the world."

Immediately a storm of abuse broke over him. The Allies and their friends in the United States were furious because he had said that their aims and those of the Germans were the same.

The German reply to Wilson's note merely proposed a conference. The Allies wanted, in general terms, restitution, reparation, recognition of the rights of small nations, and guarantee for the future. The differences in the objective of the belligerents became evident and the Allied cause was placed in a strong strategic position. The very fury of their anger at being put on a level with the Germans helped the public to understand the difference between them.

With the air alive with protests and discussions Wilson tried to straighten out a few domestic problems, to tie up a few strings that needed a tighter knot to stand the coming strain; but he was thwarted by Congress and the Senate. And the country was not yet strongly united in sentiment. Some believed that his pacifism was not sincere enough to cope with the military. Others cried, "Would God we had a man for our leader!"

Wilson simply did not hear them. Criticism, to which he was usually over-sensitive, he was now entirely indifferent to. "What can I do to assuage the fires of war?" That was his only thought. For the last time he appealed to reason, made his final plea for mediation. On January 22, 1917, in an address before the Senate he laid down the principles on which a permanent peace must be founded; and a permanent peace was the only kind of peace to be contemplated.

". . . In every discussion of the peace that must end this war," he said, "it is taken for granted that that peace must be followed by some definite concert of power which will make it virtually impossible that any such catastrophe should ever overtake us again. Every lover of mankind, every sane and thoughtful man must take that for granted. . . .

"It is inconceivable that the people of the United States should play no part in that great enterprise. . . .

"That service is nothing less than this, to add their authority and their power to the authority and force of other nations to guarantee peace and justice throughout the world. . . .

"The present war must first be ended. . . . The treaties and agreements which bring it to an end must embody terms which will create a peace that is worth guaranteeing and preserving, a peace that will win the approval of mankind, not merely a peace that will serve the several interests and immediate aims of the nations engaged. . . . If the peace presently to be made is to endure, it must be a peace made secure by the organized force of mankind.

". . . There must be, not balance of power, but a continuity of power; not organized rivalries, but an organized common peace. . . .

" They imply, first of all, that it must be a peace without victory. It is not pleasant to say this. I beg that I may be permitted to put my own interpretation upon it. . . . Victory would mean peace forced upon the loser, a victor's terms forced upon the vanquished. It would be accepted in humiliation, under duress, at an intolerable sacrifice, and would leave a sting, a resentment, a bitter memory upon which terms of peace would rest, not permanently, but only as upon quicksand. Only a peace between equals can last. Only a peace the very principle of which is equality and common participation in a common benefit. The right state of mind, the right feeling between nations, is as necessary for a lasting peace as is the just settlement of vexed questions of territory or of racial and national allegiance.

" The equality of nations upon which peace must be founded if it is to last must be an equality of rights. . . .

" And there is a deeper thing involved than even equality of rights among organized nations. No peace can last, or ought to last, which does not recognize and accept the principle that governments derive all their just powers from the consent of the governed, and that no right anywhere exists to hand people about from sovereignty to sovereignty as if they were property. . . . Any peace which does not recognize and accept this principle will inevitably be upset. . . .

" So far as practicable, moreover, every great people struggling towards a full development of its resources and of its powers should be assured a direct outlet to the great highways of the sea. . . . The freedom of the seas is the *sine qua non* of peace, equality and coöperation. . . .

"There can be no sense of safety and equality among the nations if great predominating armaments are henceforth to continue here and there to be built up and maintained. . . . The question of armaments, whether on land or sea, is the most immediately and intensely practical question connected with the future fortunes of nations and of mankind. . . .

"I would fain believe that I am speaking for the silent mass of mankind everywhere who have as yet no place or opportunity to speak their real hearts out concerning the death and ruin they see to have come already upon the persons and homes they hold most dear. . . .

"These are American principles, American policies. We could stand for no others. And they are also principles and policies of forward-looking men and women everywhere, of every modern nation, of every enlightened community. They are the principles of mankind and must prevail."

On the very brink of our entrance into the war Wilson turns and gives the reasoned, unimpassioned thought of a lifetime; and, with wonderful insight, lays down the necessary conditions for a permanent peace and the principles on which they rest in order that nations might live together in amity. The present condition of the world is a complete confirmation of his ideas.

Germany's reply to Wilson's proposals was the declaration that ruthless submarine warfare would be resumed on February 18th. She hoped by this means to starve England into submission. Secretary Zimmermann said to Ambassador Gerard: "Give us two months of this kind of warfare and we shall end the war and make peace within three months." But Germany would graciously permit the United States to send a weekly ship to England under prescribed conditions.

The President promptly directed Lansing to hand Bernstoff his passport and to recall Gerard from Berlin. Diplomatic relations with Germany were thus broken.

The time for Wilson's second inauguration was now approaching. No President has looked forward to taking the oath of office under blacker skies. Every step he was taking to prepare the country was defeated by the Senate. His request for power to arm American merchantmen was blocked by a filibuster in the Senate. This called from the President a statement in which he listed much important legislation that had been prevented and added, " A little group of wilful men, representing no opinion but their own, have rendered the great Government of the United States helpless and contemptible."

The outgoing Congress was aggressively unsympathetic. Wilson was abused and derided by the Republican members and the machine Democrats, and denounced by the Germans abroad. It would seem that in his immense struggle he stood alone when, on March 4th, he took the oath of office.

When one reads his first inaugural address and then his second, one realizes that the same spirit animated both. In the violent changes of standards that had occurred in four years he had only lifted his standard to a broader plane. In 1913 to make his country safe for democracy seemed within his power. In 1917, his constructive domestic work halted, he adjusted his step to meet the change of " time and fate "; but the ideal that took possession of him when a boy was only adhered to with increasing tenacity; then it was America, now it was the world, that should be made safe for democracy. "We are," he said in his second inaugural, "provincials no longer. The tragical events of the thirty months of vital turmoil through which we have just passed have made us citizens of the world. . . . And yet we are not less Americans on that account. We shall be the more American if we remain true to the principles in which we have been bred. . . ."

Germany put her plans into operation. American ships were sunk and American lives lost. The immense patience of the President was exhausted and his heroic efforts to keep us out of war were futile. On April 2nd the President appeared before a joint session of Congress to recommend that body to declare that a state of war existed between the United States and Germany. An immense crowd filled the House of Representatives; the air was tense with hardly suppressed excitement. On the floor were members of the House and the Senate, the Diplomatic Corps, the Cabinet and the Supreme Court. Because of expected trouble from pacifists who had massed about the Capitol, the President was escorted to the House by a body of cavalry. As he entered a burst of applause greeted him. When he said, "There is one choice we cannot make, we are incapable of making; we will not choose the path of submission and suffer the most sacred rights of our Nation and our people to be ignored or violated. The wrongs against which we now array ourselves are no common wrongs; they cut to the very roots of human life. . . . I advise that Congress declare the recent course of the Imperial German Government to be in fact nothing less than war against the Government and people of the United States," his hearers rose in enthusiastic accord. The applause was led by Chief Justice White, tears streaming down his face, absolutely overcome in his joy that this country was no longer neutral in thought or word or deed.

As the audience became quiet, the President spoke of the "mobilization of all the material resources of the country," and declared his approval of universal liability to service, of meeting the expense of the war as far as possible by a well-conceived plan of taxation. He felt that the country should be protected from inflation when vast sums had to be obtained. He emphasized again that the quarrel was not with the German people, but with their government, and that this was a war for the rights of humanity. . . . "Our motive will not be revenge or the victorious assertion of the physical might of the nation, but only the vindication of right, of human right, of which we are only a single champion. . . . We have no selfish ends to serve. We desire no conquest, no dominion. . . . We shall be satisfied when those rights have been made as secure as the faith and the freedom of nations can make them."

And behind him the President had the great mass of the plain people. His notes and addresses, the explosions and burnings of munition factories due to German agents, the criminal conspiracies against our country, in which even the German and the Austro-Hungarian embassies were involved, the ruthless sinkings of neutral ships with drownings of women and children, even attacks on hospital ships, and finally the attempt, revealed by the Zimmermann note, to incite Mexico to attack us on the south with American territory held out as bait: all these things convinced the people, many German-Americans among them, that we must fight and destroy the autocratic German government. Wilson no longer feared a divided country. To Europe came an amazed realization that the derided phrases, "peace without victory," "too proud to fight," "watchful waiting," had been the words of a great statesman, not of an emotionalist. But the man beneath the statesman suffered an agony that only those who knew him personally could realize. Hatred of war was bred in him and he was to lead his country into one that was for the masses he loved almost a mechanical piece of brutality. But the country rose with abandon; at last natural instincts were to have full play. Wilson's words of high idealism could now be borne, even with satisfaction, by the militant East; they were like a many-coloured banner to lead advancing troops. War in its actuality had become almost a forgotten evil to the older men; to the youth of the land it was a glorious unknown adventure.

Throughout this change of feeling in the country, Wilson remained unchanged. He was not an idealist where war was concerned; he was a realist who saw it always as a horror that could not be mitigated. The people were carried away by the thrill of excitement; to fight for the honour of their country — that they understood, and into dull lives came glow and colour. Wilson stood apart. "Peace without victory," — before those words, glory and triumph turned gray and cold. No wonder the people resented their stern realism. It has taken us until today to understand their full meaning and to realize the wisdom of the man who spoke them. We know now what the moral effect of war with the spoils to the victor has had upon the world.

Late in the night before Wilson's address to Congress, Frank Cobb, of the *World*, saw him. Cobb noticed how worn and white he looked, that he talked freely of all the disasters that follow the steps he was forced to take to avoid greater disasters. " He was uncanny that night. Wilson had no illusions; the panorama of the war and its end seemed to be passing before his eyes. He knew how passions were engendered by war; how the brutal feelings of the soldiers were stimulated to make them fight more fiercely. And he knew that revenge would lead the victors to impose impossible burdens upon the vanquished, which would eventually lead to another war. All the great nations except America were in the war and he had hoped we might remain without passion and be able to bring about a just and permanent peace at the proper time. But these hopes were gone; we also would have passions inflamed and there would be no nation unimpassioned and without prejudice to bring about a just and lasting peace. In his great suffering he exclaimed, ' If there is any alternative, for God's sake, let's take it! ' So far as he knew he had considered every loophole of escape and as fast as they were discovered Germany deliberately blocked them with some new outrage."

" How solemnly," he said later to me, " life is like the tide; so little of all we do is left on the shore; the backward surge of civilization seems inevitable." Then he braced himself for a greater effort; he recalled through what dreadful gales the United States had become a Union; that at least had remained from the wreckage of the Civil War; and now, out of this world wreckage, perhaps some code to prevent future wars might emerge.

That was Wilson's thought; but the country was tired of thinking; it was for action. It was to be youth's day of self-renunciation, only they did not anticipate it as such. A young Englishman had come over to help in the development of our airship plans. He had been in the second instalment of the First English Expeditionary Force; he was one of three officers of his regiment who survived, and that only because illness sent them home and saved them from shrapnel. What struck him most in the States was the ignorance of the men of what they were entering upon; they were starting for France in the spirit of football players. In Europe men went to war bravely, as a matter of course, unquestioningly, even willingly; but they knew what was ahead of them. Before me are two photographs of the same man, one of a youth consciously proud of his first uniform, handsome, gay; the other after the armistice, a defeated man.

Wilson, on the night of vigil before entering the war, saw just such human ruins, morbidly perhaps, with every sensitive nerve of his mind tortured. These moments of discouragement were, however, of short duration. After we went into the war his mind took with increasing force its natural trend; he was absorbed in the fate of humanity rather than that of individuals.

When the declaration of war was finally made, one of the greatest advocates for peace the world has ever known, together with his pacifist Secretary of War, in their plans for waging war to end wars, outdid the military. If it had to be done, then the quicker it was over the better. A year later Wilson said that Germany relied on force, and "there is, therefore, but one response possible from us: Force, Force to the uttermost. Force without stint or limit."

To his good fortune, Newton D. Baker was his Secretary of War. Human and kindly, in entire accord with the President's policies, he took the world as it came. It is a temptation to dwell long on the man who, of all others, most lightened the President's war work. He proved a great executive. The President left the management of the war to him. Though Baker kept in close communication with the President, he consulted him only on general matters of policy and not on executive details. When Baker had selected Pershing as Commander-in-Chief of military operation in France, he gave him a free hand. It was the first time in the history of the United States that war was taken out of politics. A difficult situation arose when Roosevelt wanted to take a large number of volunteers over to France under his command. But for Baker's common sense Wilson might have yielded. It was a request that both wanted to grant, and that both knew would be folly to grant. And General Wood? Many military men felt that he outclassed Pershing and thought it a mistake not to send him to France. That may be; but if so there was the prior mistake of putting Pershing in command, and Baker would send no one over that Pershing did not want. So, at the very start, they had to offend two men whom the United States loved and admired, and who, if offended, had unsurpassed powers of retaliation. Roosevelt and Wood disliked Wilson intensely and despised Baker. Wilson, in many ways, admired Roosevelt and felt his charm. He understood the force of his desire and was troubled, not annoyed by Roosevelt's hatred. Baker was rather amused by what they said of him, sorry they could not have what they wanted — he truly wished they could, but it was now Pershing's business and the decision lay with him.

There were a number of persons about the President anxious to give him freedom for the consideration of large policies, notably, his Secretary of War, Baker; his Secretary of the Treasury, McAdoo; his Secretary of Agriculture, Houston; his close friend, Colonel House; and, one of the most level-headed men in the Senate, Carter Glass.

They worked harmoniously and relieved the President of much detail.

One afternoon during the strenuous executive days before our men had gone over to France, the President ran up the steps of my house and flung himself into a chair in my library. The bottom of the chair gave way; he sprang up laughing. Looking ruefully at the chair he said, " Is this an omen that all the things I had to tell you are going to ground? " I said, " You know, Cleveland sat in that chair and remained firm." " Madam," he replied, " are you trying to remind me of Cleveland's common sense and to show me that it is the only thing that holds firm? Then let me tell you that never was there a more practical or more common-sensible thing than my derided words, ' A Peace without Victory ' and ' A League of Nations that will prevent wars.' " He drew up another chair and talked eagerly of all that was in his mind. Before he left I asked him to see an old relative who was spending the last days of his life with me, and who was very near his end. He had, when a young boy, gone into the Confederate army and his mind was filled with his experiences as a soldier under Lee. I had hung a portrait of Lee over the mantel and placed his reclining chair where he could always look up and see it; and near him I had placed his sword so that he might touch it from time to time. As the President entered the room and bent over his chair, the old soldier's eyes filled with tears; he pointed to the portrait of Lee and then, trembling, drew from his pocket, yellow with age, a letter from Washington. " I shall," he said, " put the clasp of your hand with my memory of Lee and my reverence for Washington, who was, Mr. President, my great-great uncle. You will not think a dying man a flatterer when I say you are the greatest Democratic President since the days of Washington, who was, sir, a Democrat — damn these Republicans! " The President took his hand gently with a little whimsical smile. " We won't mention aloud," he said, " about your kinsman being a Democrat; our enemies might want to argue that; and we won't damn them, for they are as anxious to beat the Kaiser as we are." What more he said I do not know, for it was said in a smiling whisper; I only know that, for a moment, the old soldier's face grew radiant. As we left the room I said, " You have given him his last great pleasure on earth, for they tell me he can only live a few days." The President's face grew sad. " Did you notice," he said, " that he was fingering his sword when we left? What we want is a different enthusiasm to satisfy the soul — but I dare not think these things now; they break my heart, and the moment's practical work is stupendous. Tell me of a good detective tale."

As the President was leaving my house a little coloured boy, with a bundle of newspaper extras, passed by shouting: " There ain't gwine to be no war; Mr. President tell Mr. Kaiser he got to stop. War done bust." " Is that," I laughingly asked the astounded President, " the voice of the people? " And he answered, " Upon my word, I believe it is. If the politicians and the potentates, all of us, handed the whole business over to that little chap we would have peace in twenty-four hours."

The stupendous work the President and his Secretary of War had on their hands was to transform a great civilian nation into a military camp. Few felt that it could be done adequately, but it was; the entire nation gave itself without stint, and the United States became an example of modern American efficiency at its height. The War Secretary and the President together were surprising; for, while the machinery of war was speeding up, the President's campaign for ending the war was never out of sight to him, nor out of sound to the world.

The first step was to draft nearly a million men for military training. Many thought the draft would be resisted with riot and bloodshed all over the country. On the contrary, it became effective without a protest; the mass of people were whole-heartedly supporting the government. During the period between our declaration of war and the actual fighting by our troops in 1918 the United States was filled with activities on a colossal scale. Boards and commissions were organized to develop and unify the industries of the country. They included the ablest men of the nation, who gave their unstinted energies to their tasks. Frederick Palmer, in his biography of Newton D. Baker, gives an illuminating account of these activities. One sees the mammoth war machine as it turns out fuel, food, arms, armament, ammunition, explosives, ships on the sea and ships in the air; cantonments, docks, railroads and hospitals built in France, etc., etc. It is a bewildering list. And within fifteen months more than two million men were transported across three thousand miles of ocean, with insignificant losses, and formed our army in France. No such feat has ever been accomplished before. And all the time the men who had conceived this plan, organized and put it over with a high conscience towards humanity and a selfless loyalty to their country, were being fought tooth and nail by their political enemies. The hatred and desires of some of these, even the most prominent, were entirely personal, while others could not comprehend acting on plans carefully formed with a thought to future generations. With them it was *me* — today — and my party, first and politicians opposed to Wilson were busy doing all in their power to upset his prestige and that of his Secretary of War. They formed a strong undercurrent determined to ruin anything or anybody, nation or man, in order to destroy Wilson. The hatred for him, led by Roosevelt and Lodge, was a consuming fire; whatever else might be done, Wilson must be destroyed. The caricatures of him became more vicious, more insolent, and the developing myth became to those who hated him, more and more infuriating. The caricature — one who believed himself the Lord's Anointed; the myth — one whom the people believed to be the Lord's Anointed; and the man — one who, " having done all that a man could, suffered all that a man must."

In 1918 animosity towards the government was at its height. Prominent politicians felt outraged that they were not consulted, that they were being kept in the dark as to what was being done. But it was imperative that the plans of the government should be kept secret unless the enemy also was to be informed. Things reached a climax when a number, headed by Roosevelt, actually wanted to form a war cabinet and take the conduct of the war out of the hands of the President, declaring that the country was being ruined by Wilson, and that only such a robust fighter as Roosevelt could save it. They cried out that nothing was being done. Then Baker gave the alarmed in the country a little glimpse of what the government was doing; and Wilson sent for Stetinius, a man whom all the country trusted, and asked him to examine carefully the work of the Department of War and advise any improvements he thought ought to be made. He reported that there was too much red tape required by the law and too many in control, that the laws should be revised and control put under one head. Then the President demanded of Congress the powers of a dictator, just what Roosevelt's war cabinet had advocated but to a greater degree, and Wilson became at once the central figure of the world; nothing could be done without considering him. To use force without limit was his purpose in order to end the war; but he was always looking ahead, seeing the end, determined to establish everywhere the conviction that the government was for the benefit of the people, not the people for the government.

In an address to the two houses of Congress on January 8, 1918, after alluding to the willingness of the Central Powers to end the war on their own terms, he put in concrete language the conditions for peace which he had expressed to the Senate in more general terms on January 22, 1917.

"We entered this war because violations of right had occurred which touched us to the quick and made the life of our own people impossible unless they were corrected and the world secured once for all against their recurrence. What we demand in this war, therefore, is nothing peculiar to ourselves. . . . All the peoples of the world are in effect partners in this interest. . . . The program of the world's peace, therefore, is our program, and that program, the only possible program, as we see it, is this:

"I. Open covenants of peace, openly arrived at, after which there shall be no private international understandings of any kind but diplomacy shall proceed always frankly and in the public view.

"II. Absolute freedom of navigation upon the seas, outside territorial waters, alike in peace and in war, except as the seas may be closed in whole or in part by international action for the enforcement of international covenants.

"III. The removal, so far as possible, of all economic barriers and the establishment of an equality of trade conditions among all the nations consenting to the peace and associating themselves for its maintenance.

"IV. Adequate guarantees given and taken that national armaments will be reduced to the lowest point consistent with domestic safety.

"V. A free, open-minded, and absolutely impartial adjustment of all colonial claims, based upon a strict observance of the principle that in determining all such questions of sovereignty the interests of the populations concerned must have equal weight with the equitable claims of the government whose title is to be determined.

"VI–XIII. [These sections cover the evacuation of Russian territory, the evacuation and restoration of Belgian and French territory, the return of Alsace-Lorraine, the readjustment of national boundaries and the erection of new States.]

"XIV. A general association of nations must be formed under specific covenants for the purpose of affording mutual guarantees of political independence and territorial integrity to great and small States alike.

". . . For such arrangements and covenants we are willing to fight and to continue to fight until they are achieved; but only because we wish the right to prevail and desire a just and stable peace such as can be secured only by removing the chief provocation to war, which this program does remove. . . . An evident principle runs through the whole program I have outlined. It is the principle of justice to all peoples and nationalities, and their right to live on equal terms of liberty and safety with one another, whether they be strong or weak."

His first point has been generally misunderstood and derided, but in a letter to Lansing, March 12, 1918, he explained: "When I pronounced for open diplomacy I meant not that there should be no private discussions of delicate matters, but that no secret agreement of any sort should be entered into and that all international relations, when fixed, should be open, aboveboard and explicit."

The above are Wilson's famous Fourteen Points. His words fired the imagination of the world and all nations accepted them. Some feared, as was not unnatural, that a man who so longed for peace could not effectively wage war. But Wilson had given proof of his attitude in the address to Congress, mentioned above; and as to the Pope's proposed terms of peace in August, 1917, he would have none of it. He replied, " His Holiness in substance proposes that we return to the *status quo ante bellum*. . . . The object of this war is to deliver the free peoples of the world from the menace and actual power of a vast military establishment . . . which . . . stopped at no barrier . . . swept a whole continent within the tide of blood. . . . To deal with such power by way of peace upon the plan proposed by His Holiness would . . . involve a recuperation of its strength and a renewal of its policy. . . ."

To the oppressed throughout America and throughout the world, this declaration was the dawn of a new hope. The sacrifices that were being made were to prevent such horrors ever occurring again. One could not go anywhere and not be surprised by the impression his words had made; it was a new way of looking at war. Many felt that their sufferings would be an insurance to their grandchildren against another such war.

The war-ships were steadily developing in efficiency; our troops were being rapidly transported to France; but no one felt that Germany was conquered; she seemed still a very formidable foe. Foch and Pershing were urging the necessity of haste in sending over more American troops. The best we hoped for was that a decisive victory for the Allies would come in the summer of 1919. And when, on October 5, 1918, Germany appealed to the President for an armistice and a negotiated peace based on the Fourteen Points, the whole world was amazed. Strong in the faith of his fathers Wilson believed in conversion, but not quite so extreme a one as that from *Deutschland Ueber Alles* to his Fourteen Points. He wanted no negotiated peace and he would not be manoeuvred into a disadvantageous position. And so he asked for more definite statements of Germany's attitude. He would not treat with the Imperial rulers of Germany but only with a government controlled by the people. Being reassured on this point and having made it clear that no armistice would be considered which did not destroy Germany's ability to continue the war, and that the military conditions of an armistice would be left to the Commanders of the Allied and Associated armies, he passed the correspondence over to the Supreme War Council. On November 5th he could announce to his cabinet that the terms for an armistice had been agreed upon by the Allies. On November 11th they were signed by the Germans, and the war was over.

During this period Colonel House was in constant communication with the President. As soon as the armistice was agreed upon Wilson asked him to go to Europe as a special representative of the government of the United States and act for him in matters related to the war. Not only was the President kept informed of all the proceedings but he was given a very illuminating insight into the psychology of the men with whom later he would have to work.

Then Wilson decided to go to Europe himself and

take his place at the Peace Conference. He made known his intention of going to Europe in his annual message to the two houses of Congress on December 2nd. "I welcome this occasion," he said, "to announce to the Congress my purpose to join in Paris the representatives of the governments with which we have been associated in the war against the Central Empires for the purpose of discussing with them the main features of the treaty of peace. . . . The Allied Governments have accepted the bases of peace which I outlined to the Congress on the eighth of January last, as the Central Empires also have, and very reasonably desire my personal counsel in their interpretation and application. . . . The peace settlements which are now to be agreed upon are of transcendent importance both to us and to the rest of the world, and I know of no business which should take precedence of them. The gallant men of our armed forces on land and sea have consciously fought for the ideals which they knew to be the ideals of their country; . . . I owe it to them to see to it, so far as in me lies, that no false or mistaken interpretation is put upon them. . . . I could think of no call to service which could transcend this. . . . May I hope, Gentlemen of the Congress, that in the delicate tasks I have to perform . . . I may have the encouragement and added strength of your united support. . . ." His appeal did not fall upon sympathetic ears; and when early in December he sailed for France there were ominous political clouds in the home skies. Very ugly speeches had been made and spread about. Nevertheless, there were still people in the country who considered him little less than a god. He underestimated the politicians and saw in the adulation of the people only their desires as represented by him, their servant. He saw himself in the picture hardly at all. To read in a letter from him of the journey to France and his reception there was to have every dramatic effect wiped out; he dwelt only on his ideals. But the drama was there.

His reception in France when the *George Washington* approached the harbour and steamed between lines of American and Allied war-ships, thundering the presidential salute, was spectacular. After landing at Brest he visited cities in France, England and Italy, and received an ovation not heretofore accorded any other man. Bolitho writes: "No one ever had such cheers; I, who heard them in the streets of Paris, can never forget them in my life. I saw Foch pass, Clémenceau pass, Lloyd George, generals, returning troops, banners, but Wilson heard from his carriage something different, inhuman — or superhuman. Oh, the immovably shining, smiling man!"

It came to him overwhelmingly — the magnitude of the task of controlling the aftermath of the war. Who could satisfy the long stifled hunger for life and freedom of the downtrodden and oppressed? It was a fearful, not a triumphant moment when he saw the helpless people looking to him with the high aspirations his words had aroused in them. What was hoped for from him was a miracle; their need and his passionate desire to fulfil it threw him back to his fathers' creed — perhaps a miracle might be accomplished! But his habit of translating faith and hope into practical work was sure to assert itself; he never lingered but momentarily in a visionary atmosphere. "If I know myself," he wrote to me, "it is of my work, not myself, I am thinking."

Then the Peace Conference began its work. Wilson was selected to make the opening address at the plenary Assembly on January 25th, and he took the stand that a League of Nations was imperative to insure future peace in the world and that it must be an integral part of the Peace Treaty. The League must be the keynote of the settlement, a settlement that must satisfy the mass of the plain people. The Assembly was united in accepting these ideals, and a committee, with Wilson as chairman, was appointed to draw up a constitution for the proposed League.

The representatives of the Powers, in their moment of uncertainty, had accepted the Fourteen Points as a basis of the armistice. When victory was in their hands each represented only his own nation; and each wanted the same thing — the spoils of war and as much as he could get for his nation regardless of all else — and said so. Each felt that he knew well what was best, not for the world, but for his own country; and each was absorbed in the question of his own national boundaries. Wilson alone saw it as a whole.

As the struggle developed he knew that his Fourteen Points could not prevail except in the future; bit by bit they would be destroyed; and in their place the League of Nations was the world's best hope. It would not only prevent future wars but in time would bring to light the Fourteen Points which now were growing so dim. Through it the world would keep faith with the people.

The first draft of the Covenant of the League was completed, and was accepted by the Conference on February 14th. The Paris *Daily Mail* commented: "It was impossible to listen to the document which President Wilson read, to his comments upon it and to the declarations of the Allied representatives, without feeling that the affairs of the world were being lifted into new dimensions. The old dimensions of national individualism . . . were raised, if only for an instant, to a higher plane. . . . How long will the instant last? No man can say. All that can be said is that yesterday a sense that something new, something irrevocable, pervaded the Conference Hall. . . ."

The next day, Wilson, very much encouraged, sailed for the United States to be present during the final sessions of Congress.

He was not aware of the adverse fate ahead of him as he left Paris amid the enthusiastic *au revoir* of the populace and the dignitaries. The applause, he thought, was for his hard-fought-for League, and he was therefore very hopeful.

Why he steadily believed the people in his own country were with him is hard to understand. It has been said that when he went to Versailles he had, as it were, to fight the beasts at Ephesus, but they were tame creatures compared with his own countrymen. If his influence had not been steadily undermined at home, a far better peace would have been possible. High idealization, unselfish aims, were given by him as representing his country; and even as he talked, notes and propaganda from his political enemies, denying that he represented America, found their way across the Atlantic, greatly bewildering his colleagues. What was this America which Wilson idealized and which seemed to discredit him? When Englishmen speak, they are England; Frenchmen are France; Italians are Italy; but Americans did not seem to be America.

America only was the unknown quantity, and unfortunately in 1919 she was far from idealistic. On the top wave financially, she set out to repudiate the League, and was to lose for herself a great position. It is not a stretch of the imagination to believe that it was the moment when she might have become in reality the greatest nation on earth.

Wilson's address when he landed in Boston shows his

enthusiastic belief in the success of the League and his country's interest in it. The support of America is essential. " America is the hope of the world. And if she does not justify that hope, results are unthinkable. Men will be thrown back upon bitterness of disappointment not only but bitterness of despair. All nations will be set up as hostile camps again. . . ."

He found the strongest kind of opposition in the Senate, led by Lodge, and it went so far that the Senate would not attend to anything else, not even to the necessary business of the government.

As soon as Congress adjourned the President left Washington for Paris. At New York he and former President Taft spoke from the same platform in favour of the League. The President's address was much like his address in Boston: The League is necessary to preserve the peace of the world; and America's support is essential. He left the country a sick man — badgered, indignant, believing that the men opposing the League were not voicing America. He determined to fight to the end.

The question often comes up: Would it have been wiser for the President not to have taken his second trip to Paris? The arguments persuading him to remain at home, " a mystery," " a god on the mountain," to whom appeal must be made from a distance, offended him. It is strange that any one knowing him even slightly could think it would be possible to arouse in him a personal vanity — he had none. Were he to be taken up to a high mountain and shown all the material possessions and personal honours in the world, he would have experienced no temptation. But to make the world safe for democracy! That did tempt him. He felt he knew how it should be done — failing a miracle — by practical intelligence. The only question he considered was whether his presence or absence would best help his objects; and he was convinced that he could be more effective in Paris than in Washington. Clémenceau, Lloyd George, Orlando: he saw in them only obstacles or helps to the League, and he was not deceived by their diplomacy. He forced the League on them by his personality and imperative urge. Without him it would have been dropped at almost any point of the road. For the sake of uniting the world in one constructive purpose he would have given his life.

On his return to Europe the Covenant of the League was at once taken up and the unraveling of the Fourteen Points was continued amid much dispute. No doubt among the influences persuading him not to deliver an ultimatum and go home, but to compromise, must be reckoned his own dread of a revolutionary movement in the war-stricken countries if the conference should end in failure. Russia was an object lesson to him; he had never been a radical.

To mention the many questions in the Conference is not only impossible, but would be futile. To the world at large the Conference was correctly visualized as an arena of hate, and no one would elect to take the post of umpire. In the final scene we see what it has all meant and means: The stage, Versailles; the Commission, seated, waiting to deliver to the German delegates their country's doom. When the Germans are brought in before their conquerors, Count Brockdorff-Rantzau, broken, bitter, keeps his seat as Clémenceau, standing, hands him the treaty; in his person France expresses her revenge for innumerable injuries inflicted upon her by Germany. She has taken her revenge, but in taking it she has left the figure of Brockdorff-Rantzau ominously impressive. As he sat there in his fury of humiliation and uttered his words of denunciation, the hell war throws us into fairly seethed in the air. Wilson sat looking at him, his soul burning in his eyes. Was this his " peace without victory? " His agony on realizing that the Germans looked upon him as a victor almost broke his heart. His mind, he said later, went back by contrast to a scene in his own country when Grant returned to Lee his surrendered sword. After the Treaty had been given the Germans all compromise died in the American President. He had compromised as regards the terms of the Treaty, but now he was done with compromise. Colonel House, in his *Intimate Papers*, speaks of urging the President to meet the Senate in a conciliatory spirit. The reply was: " House, I have found that one can never get anything in this life that is worth while without fighting for it." He had done all he could. From now on, no compromise!

X

A WORLD TRAGEDY

. . . . Have not I
. . . . .
Broken my body for a cause,
In a lost field, lost land?
There is no word in any tongue,
Can make clear to one or all,
My strange hunger, or that fight
My back against the wall.

Lizette Woodsworth Reese

Chapter Ten

A WORLD TRAGEDY

THE day after signing the Treaty Wilson sailed for the United States to enter upon his struggle for the League. In spite of his determination to fight uncompromisingly, his desire for its success made him throw into every discussion an immense patience. How great the patience and how desperate the struggle, which cost him his life, we can only surmise.

The Treaty was universally condemned and Wilson with it. Too much had been expected. The people of the Allied nations had been promised full reparations from Germany, but it was not possible to satisfy them. New States were set up and attempts made to fix their boundaries in accordance with social, racial, religious and economic conditions, but these conditions were not compatible with each other. In America some wanted milder terms for Germany; some, more drastic. Wilson had slowly been convinced that a just treaty could not be made; he combined the League inextricably with the Treaty, believing that, given time, it would modify the faults of the latter and would be an obstacle to future wars. His mind was bent on a broad policy, world-wide, as important for America as for Europe. He represented neither Democrats nor Republicans; he was supported by prominent men of both parties, such as Taft, Root, Wickersham, Eliot, Lowell and many others. Even a majority of the Senate were in favour of the Treaty. But there were politicians in both parties against him.

The aftermath of the Civil War and that of the World War were much the same; the difference was only that the one was world-wide, the other localized. Lincoln sought a just and lasting peace between the States, and his untimely assassination came from the bitterness of those he alone could have helped, the bitterness brought about by fanaticism, malice and greed. Andrew Johnson attempted to follow Lincoln's policies and was bitterly fought by the politicians led by Thaddeus Stevens and Charles Sumner, again incited by desire of political advantage, by malice, greed and revenge. Wilson, coming upon this scene in his youth, looked upon all around him with unclouded eyes. He absorbed the genius of Lincoln's thought, made it part of himself, and set to work to bring it to life by balanced statesmanship; his " peace without victory " was merely paraphrasing Lincoln's " with malice towards none; with charity for all; with firmness in the right, as God gives us to see the right, let us strive on to finish the work we are in; to bind up the nation's wounds . . . to do all that may achieve and cherish a just and lasting peace among ourselves and with all nations." To this idealism Wilson, later in his life, added his Fourteen Points and the League of Nations, and we have the heart and genius of Lincoln and the trained mind of Wilson united. The year 1919 was a replica on a grand scale of the year 1865.

Wilson was venomously repudiated by self-seeking politicians in his own country and by revengeful victors abroad. Lloyd George wrote: " I believe I may say that never have I seen such vicious, cruel vituperation as was heaped upon him at home and in Paris at the time of the Peace Conference."

The European statesmen never doubted the moral greatness of Wilson after his presence with them at the Conference. The late Sir Geoffrey Butler, Conservative member of Parliament for Cambridge, said to the writer, " One by one I have spoken to those who were at the Conference and it is always the same answer: ' The Conference was Wilson; and, if his country had not been unable to appreciate him, a great victory for world peace would have been won.' " That was true only in part. The Conference was Wilson in ways they did not comprehend and would not have followed if they had comprehended them. They saw his genuineness, they realized the greatness of the man; but they could not grasp that he actually believed that they would live up to the Fourteen Points. Each representative at the Conference knew that his country would not stand back of him in any effort for a just peace. It was impossible; the people of Europe had been led to look upon revenge and slaughter as the highest form in which to interpret patriotism. They had endured untold suffering and their countries had been practically wrecked; they would now have their revenge. France, England, Italy, intended to crush Germany, and they did. With all America's sins, and they are many, she is by no means wholly responsible for Wilson's defeat at Versailles.

Wilson underestimated the power of the politicians in America. Incredible as it may seem he was hopeful when he left Paris for the United States. He fully believed that he could persuade the country to accept the League, and nothing short of death could induce him to give up the struggle for its acceptance. The politicians had started a fire with which they intended to consume every scrap of Wilson's policies; they had the fuel to feed it — prosperity.

Wilson thought he could light a stronger flame with the torch of self-sacrifice.

When he found that he could not bring the necessary two-thirds of the Senate to accept the Treaty and the League, he decided to appeal to the people; and against the protests of his physician, his wife and his friends, he started on a trip across the continent, speaking at many places. He knew he was risking his life, but he thought he was doing no more than the soldiers who had fought in the trenches. And no one could stop him. His addresses were all devoted to explanations and defence of the League. He was received enthusiastically at some places, indifferently at others. His enemies were not idle; he was followed by a group of Senators, trying to counteract whatever effect his addresses might have made. They and other politicians played on the credulity and prejudices of the people, especially the German-Americans and Irish-Americans. And the general demoralization of a coming election was in the air.

Those who saw Wilson before he started on his Western tour tell how shockingly ill he looked, and the news, when it came, that he had broken down and was being rushed back to Washington, surprised no one who had seen him. His daughter, Margaret, who had heard alarming accounts of his illness, met the presidential train when it arrived in Washington and was greatly relieved when she saw her father. He walked with her to his car and talked quite casually of his breakdown, almost as if he felt that, with a little rest, all danger was over. But on reaching the White House he quickly showed strain. The gay life and talk about him were too much; and after a few days' effort to resume his usual routine he suffered a severe stroke. From this time his political life was over, he was

WOODROW WILSON
From the bust by Harriet Frishmuth

a desperately ill man, kept alive only by his amazing vitality and will. His mind was perfectly clear but he was physically unable to do more than hold in his grip the determination to carry over the League of Nations; if it died he died with it. In a sense he was already dead, and his opponents were only fighting to drag from a dead hand and kill the living idea which it held in its grasp. It is distressing to consider the last years of his official life. We are watching a man on a rack, the screw turned by the people of his own nation, for which he so selflessly fought. He would never give in, nor would they; and the result was inevitable.

No concrete example in the history of our country has so clearly shown the flaw in our Constitution as that which was illustrated during the slow death of Woodrow Wilson. We are like people living in a costly frame dwelling, which holds all our possessions, uninsured. Among the defects in our Constitution, Wilson once said, certainly one of the greatest is the status of our Vice-President. He has no important part in the government, he is not a member of the Cabinet, and may be out of sympathy with the policies of the President. It is only in case of the death or total disability of the latter that he becomes important; then he becomes President — a man who has been selected largely on geographical considerations to strengthen the party ticket at the election, with no assurance of qualifications for the office that may come to him by accident. This idiotic arrangement, which Wilson had so deplored, subjected him to much unjust criticism. He was too ill to see his Cabinet except upon rare occasions, and the United States was left leaderless.

No one would have seen the insecurity of Wilson's position more clearly than he had it befallen another man, but he had gone through so much suffering in his life, and in spite of it, had kept his hand on the helm, that he felt he could spur his jaded body to successful action. And those about him could not fail to catch some of his spirit — they had so often seen him accomplish the seemingly impossible.

Wilson, the man, was devotedly looked after and all his physical needs supplied; but his political needs were construed for him and for the country by amateurs. Important questions were met, as was thought best, by people whose ideals were not in the least his, and who were untrained in governmental matters. The arraignment is not against those in control in the White House; they acted only as the majority of devoted families would have acted. The arraignment is against our Constitution that permits such a confused state of affairs.

His wife and physicians were confronted with the task of keeping from him serious worries, and at the same time of making it seem that he was apparently in control of the government. All manner of rumours about the cause and the extent of his breakdown were circulated, and his Cabinet was kept for some time entirely in the dark. Houston, in his *Eight Years with Wilson's Cabinet*, after mentioning his apprehension on hearing of the President's breakdown, writes, " There was no direct or authoritative word of any sort even to members of the Cabinet from the White House or from the physician. . . . We canvassed the matter among ourselves but none of us could furnish any light." On October 3rd, he saw Secretary Baker, who said, " I am scared literally to death." He looked it. The next day Tumulty told him confidentially that the President " ' was paralyzed in one leg and one arm.' He expressed great alarm over the situation. We agreed that it would be one of the tragedies of the ages if the President was incapacitated." The next day Houston found the Vice-President in a great state of worry and some indignation. " He asked me if I could give him the real facts, which I was unable to do. I could not even repeat what had been told me, because it had been said in confidence. The Vice-President expressed the view that he ought immediately to be informed; that it would be a tragedy for him to assume the duties of President, at best; and that it would be equally a tragedy for the people; that he knew many men who knew more about the affairs of the government than he did, and that it would be especially trying for him if he had to assume the duties without warning. He showed resentment that the doctors were keeping the situation a mystery so far as he especially was concerned." Alarming rumours went about that the President was worse, and Lansing called a meeting of the Cabinet. When they met, " Lansing said that it was necessary to decide whether or not we should continue to carry on the Government — that there was nothing to guide us as to who would decide the question of the ability of the President to discharge the duties of his office." After discussing the situation they decided to send for Dr. Grayson and ask him to give them a statement of the President's condition. " Dr. Grayson stated that the President's condition had improved over Sunday, but that he could not say when he would be out of danger — that the scales might tip either way. He added that they might tip the wrong way, especially if he was harassed by business matters, and that he should be bothered as little as possible. He told us that the President's mind was very clear, but that he was suffering from a nervous breakdown, from indigestion and a depleted system."

Under such conditions it is not surprising that many things that were done during his illness seemed unlike him and caused offence. His request for Lansing's resignation was ill-timed. Lansing had not been in accord with the President's policies, but the reason given for requesting his resignation was not convincing — merely that he had called a Cabinet meeting without being authorized to do so by the President. Houston writes: "I was surprised not that Lansing was asked to resign, but that he should have been at that time. From what I have heard, the question was raised in my mind why he had not been asked sooner." The papers made much of it.

Wilson's mind was always centred on what he felt was most essential; now his thoughts were wholly fixed on the League. Consequently it was unfortunate that Colonel House, his right hand man in regard to the League, could not see or communicate with him. In their last effort to put through the League of Nations they should have been together. It was not only like changing horses in midstream, but changing them when the current was swiftest. Colonel House is convinced that if he could have reached the President either personally or through his letters, the League with a few reservations would have passed the Senate. He knew that the reason Wilson refused any compromise came from his entire distrust of Lodge and his colleagues. This distrust seems to have been justified by an incident related by Dodd in his book, *Woodrow Wilson and His Work:* ". . . a member of that body the Senate said to a constituent in Maine, Wilson might draw a great treaty, propose a world peace that was without flaw, but the Republicans would never allow his work to succeed. 'That,' said a Senator, 'was decreed before he went to Paris.' The Senate had brow beaten Cleveland eight years; it had driven John Hay to resign from the McKinley cabinet; and it had refused to assent to most of the best measures of the Roosevelt presidency. How could it now forego the chance to break one leader whose career had been and still was a reminder that some things were not right in the country? The bitterest of the opposition leaders hardened their hearts and the more moderate stiffened their necks; all chances must be taken. Wilson must be broken."

It was to be expected that a breach with Colonel House would be reported: he had not been called to the White House, Wilson had turned against him, the Colonel's letters had been left unanswered — *etc., etc.* It was the old gossip that had followed their friendship for years past, which, as a rule, they had met with silent contempt. Now circumstances kept them apart; but his daughter, Margaret, told me that her father's affection for Colonel House had remained unchanged. And Colonel House assures me that his feeling for the President has never wavered. If any of the gossip came to Wilson's ears it failed to disturb him. He knew his friends and they knew him. But now he was ill he could not reach them; and every bit of strength he had was absorbed in his last struggle for the League.

From the many malicious stories with which the campaigners were filling the air I narrate two because they illustrate Wilson's attitude towards his friends, and theirs towards him.

The episode which seems to have broken his friendship with his secretary, Tumulty, has never been correctly given, though of political propaganda and melodramatic nonsense there has been abundance. Just before the Jackson Day dinner (1920), Wilson's daughter writes me, Tumulty came to Wilson and begged that he would sign a statement endorsing Cox's candidacy for the presidential nomination. This Wilson flatly and categorically refused to do, as he had decided not to endorse any one. The morning after the dinner there appeared a statement in *The*

Times saying that Wilson had endorsed Cox. Wilson immediately wrote to the paper that he had not made the endorsement; he did not know at the time that Tumulty had sent the statement to the paper. On learning this the President said, "If I had known it was Tumulty I should have been silent and let the matter pass, because of his affection for me and mine for him. My affection for him is still unchanged, but now I have given the denial I cannot take it back because it is the truth." He then wrote Tumulty the kind of letter a father might write to a son whom he cared for and wanted to protect. His concern was not about the statement falsely attributed to him, but that Tumulty's responsibility for it should be known. Tumulty adored Wilson, the man; but Wilson's ideals were beyond his comprehension. Wilson understood both his love and limitations, and closed all discussion of the matter by saying, "I am sure that Tumulty's intentions were good."

In the autumn of 1919 a strike of the bituminous coal miners for higher wages threatened to cut off the coal supply of the country, and Harry A. Garfield, who had been fuel commissioner during the war, was recalled to Washington to bring about a settlement of the dispute. The President and Garfield were wholly in accord that an increase of wages should be granted the miners on account of the higher cost of living, but that this should be absorbed by the operators without raising the cost of fuel to the public. After full discussion and consideration a report was drawn up for the President, and Garfield informed him that the agreement with the miners was in accordance with his views and could be safely approved. He also suggested that an *advisory* committee be appointed to collect all pertinent information for future use. When the report came to the President it had been altered without Garfield's knowledge, and contained a recommendation that a committee of three be appointed, one representing the miners, one the operators, and one the government, with *power* to settle the questions at issue. This rendered the government helpless, as its representative could always be out-voted in the committee. On learning of this substitution Garfield immediately wrote to the President, explaining his objections to the report, and revealing the trick that had been played upon him. He was informed that the President had said, " Go ahead; I know those men." The next day, however, he received a communication from the White House, stating that the President had decided to let the report stand as it was. This took all authority and usefulness away from the fuel commissioner, and Garfield was constrained to ask that his resignation be accepted.

I was lunching with Dr. and Mrs. Garfield when the answer accepting his resignation was received, a cold, formal note, almost an insult to an old friend with whom he had been in entire agreement over the question in dispute, and who had laid aside his duties as president of Williams College in order to help the government. Handing the note to me Dr. Garfield said, " This is the kind of thing his enemies say the President does. You and I know that he does not. I am convinced that the President never saw my letter." Dr. Garfield spoke feelingly of Mrs. Wilson, of her sad and difficult position with her husband so ill; of the imperative necessity to save him from anxieties and at the same time important governmental matters to be decided.

The sordidness of the Tumulty episode is forgotten when we hear the President, in spite of the evidence, quietly saying, " I know Tumulty's affection for me. Mine for him remains unchanged. I am sure his intentions were good." And the unshakable faith of the President's friends forcibly stands out as Dr. Garfield, in spite of the evidence, quietly says, "This is the order of things his enemies say the President does. You and I know he does not."

No power could stop the disgusting gossip, the business of putting poison in other people's wells. If Wilson could have died on his Western trip, what suffering he would have been spared! But the curtain rarely drops at the right moment in actual life. Lincoln was fortunate.

It would have been amazing if the issue could have been won by Wilson, fought, as he was, by a group of clever politicians in robust health, who knew exactly what they wanted, and interpreted by a group of devoted members of his household more concerned with his physical than his political life.

Any hope for the League was over when he became ill. Sir J. J. Thomson, Master of Trinity College, Cambridge, England, writes to me: "I wish I could remember more than I can of what Arthur Balfour said about him [Wilson]. I know he admired him greatly and I remember his saying when Wilson was stricken with illness that he thought it one of the greatest tragedies of the world; for he was convinced that, if it had not occurred, he would have swung the country around and carried it with him." Knowing the country and the times it does not seem probable — for the American people had "great possessions," and wanted more.

Wilson entered the war "to make the world safe for democracy." This has all the appearance of a cant phrase, and might be compared with the way the Republican Party made the United States safe for itself for a long period after the Civil War. But that is not at all what he meant. Earlier he had said, " Our democracy, plainly, was not a body of doctrine; it was a stage of development," and its success depended on the character of the people. " It is for this that we love democracy: for the emphasis it puts on character; for the tendency to exalt the purposes of the average man to some high level of endeavour; for its just principle of common assent in matters in which all are concerned; for its ideals of duty and its sense of brotherhood." This is the democracy for which he was fighting with his back to the wall — ill, often indignant, practically helpless, but undeterred.

The Democratic Party in 1920 commanded a peculiar interest, for the problems of the world were vital. The Senate was led by as vindictive a man as ever lived, Henry Cabot Lodge, and the Treaty was rejected because its keynote was the League of Nations. It was the one small ray of hope in the world's dilemma; it would hurt the stricken man in the White House to know that he had given his life in vain, so a rejected Treaty was sent him. Wilson still said, " This is not the voice of the people. The election will show it." And the answer came when the country overwhelmingly voted for a man who neither thought nor acted, and who would never have lost a moment's sleep over an idea or an ideal. The very word " idealism " had become obnoxious. " Let us eat, drink and be merry," America cried, and forgot the end, " for tomorrow we die."

When on March 4, 1921, Warren Harding became the country's Chief Executive, a greatly conceived plan came to an end and the racket of a jazz band filled the air. Suffering the fate of most great leaders, the ex-President seemed to personify in his broken figure the ever recurring tragedy of humanity. All that in any way had uplifted the war, the great heroism and self-sacrifice, had only ended in a riot of dissipation; the politicians, not the patriots, had won. America was out for a debauch of prosperity.

To one looking at the face of Woodrow Wilson, in its unutterable sadness, as he handed over the government to Harding, a startling change seemed to have taken place. Always inseparable from the lovable man had lived a masterful leader and fighter. Involuntarily one still looked for the glint of fire in his eye, but he had yielded his sword. The struggle against overwhelming odds was over; he had met his defeat.

After the inauguration ceremonies he went to his house in S Street, where he lived for the remaining three years of his life. For a little while he was not entirely incapacitated. One of the few public functions he attended was the unveiling of the monument to the unknown soldier. It had always been difficult for him to appreciate why one should need a symbol to illustrate a thought — to him it was turning from the quick to the dead. When his car passed by in the parade, and he heard again the enthusiastic shouts of the people for him, he was overwhelmed with pity. A parade, a costly monument for the unknown dead! And the streets filled with living unknown soldiers, their lives wrecked! It was the inevitable aftermath of the war — a world tragedy.

XI
THE END

Servant of God, well done, well hast thou fought
The better fight, who single hast maintained
Against revolted multitudes the Cause
Of Truth, in word mightier than they in Armes:
And for the testimonie of Truth hast borne
Universal reproach, far worse to bear
Than violence: for this was all thy care
To stand approv'd in sight of God, though Worlds
Judg'd thee perverse:

Milton

Chapter Eleven

THE END

THE events that took place during the last years of Wilson's life are to be deplored, but they failed to move him deeply. His mind was clear, his body wrecked. Gradually the agony and bitterness of his defeat passed away. He continued to believe in the people, but more than all, in a power that moved inevitably behind events. His religion sustained him.

The warmth of his affection for his friends, his need of their response, remained unabated, unchanged. "My friends grow more and more indispensable to me," he wrote to me in the autumn of 1923. "Little as I see them I think more and more about them. . . . I must see my friends or starve." As he lay dying, his daughter Margaret wrote me: "He is longing for news of his old friends; he keeps asking for them all the time. . . . At the mention of their names he seems to come back from a long distance with expectant pleasure." He was troubled by little disturbing wreckage along the friendship road of his life. Extravagantly loved or hated, he returned love's debt with high interest. To hate he remained a debtor. There was nothing in him to respond to it.

From his daughter Margaret we have the following realistic picture of her father: "Often during those last years of his life, in the house on S Street, we used to sit together in silence. Then quietly, as if in contemplation, he would speak. At such times I felt it was his great soul speaking — not the tired body. The last time that happened was in December of the winter he died. We had been talking — then for a long time we were silent. Suddenly he said, 'I think it was best after all that the United States did not join the League of Nations.' A little startled, I said, 'Why, Father darling?' He answered, 'Because our entrance into the League at the time I returned from Europe might have been only a personal victory. Now, when the American people join the League it will be because they are convinced it is the right thing to do, and then will be the *only right* time for them to do it.' Then with a little humorous smile — 'Perhaps God knew better than I did after all.'"

It is amazing, his belief in the people. With death at his side, his daughter's letter shows how, compelled by long habit, he turned automatically, characteristically, for a moment, to lay all the travails and ideals of his life before the people, upon whose verdict the case of Woodrow Wilson and his democracy must ultimately rest.

On February 3, 1924, he died. His remains were placed in the Protestant Episcopal Cathedral of Saint John the Divine, in Washington. It is to be hoped that some day they may be carried across the ocean and rest in the temple of the League of Nations. He lived for America, but he gave his life for the peace of the world.

Though he had been so long dying, the moment of his death caused universal emotion. Kings and statesmen did him honour, flags were put at half-mast in many foreign countries, and about his door men and women of the people knelt and prayed. In an address six years later, Newton D. Baker said:

"Temporary reputations are often made quickly; great

traditions necessarily grow slowly. The ultimate view which America and the world are to take of Mr. Wilson and his contribution to our thinking and conscience will become a great tradition. Therefore, I am patient as I sit watching how it grows by annular rings like a giant forest tree."

James Truslow Adams, in his recent *March of Democracy*, writes: " He failed but he failed nobly, in perhaps the greatest effort that any statesman has ever made to bring content and lasting peace to all mankind."

The failure was humanity's. Wilson's conceptions made a profound impression upon the world, though it would not follow his ideas then, and will not now. He believed that ideals could be put into practical use and be lived, and on that rock he broke as all humanitarian idealists, who have taken Christ as their Exemplar, must break.

Gradually mankind begins to realize that the Treaty of Versailles was a vicious one; that if Wilson's lead had been accepted, a very different world would have emerged. The evils which he predicted would follow the failure of the nations to live up to their promises, and the isolation of the United States, have materialized. Wilson's doctrines of Peace Without Victory and his Fourteen Points may yet prove to be one of the great conceptions of the ages, by which nations may be able to live together in mutual tolerance. Three or four generations from now, " the stone which the builders rejected " may become " the head of the corner," a hope, not a prophecy. The fog of the present is too dense and the end of the road too far ahead.

INDEX

Index

Index

Index